Dan Johannesen
309 - 1766

NORWEGIAN MENUS
35
MASTER CHEFS SHARE THEIR SECRETS

Editor: Gunnar Jerman

These recipes have been developed in cooperation with Morten Schakenda and the Gastronomic Institute.

Food photographer: Bengt Wilson

English translation and recipe adaptation: Melody Favish

Index Publishing A/S

Flyleaf: Top-quality ingredients from the oceans, lakes, mountains and forests form the foundation for the Norwegian restaurant kitchen. Pictures such as this were not at all commonplace in Norway when Bjørn Winsnes took this one for W. Køltzow A/S in 1978.

Nussfjord is one of the most charming fishing villages in the Lofoten Islands. The old cabins, where fishermen spent a few slightly less chilly hours indoors between their stints in open boats at sea, have been transformed into lodging for tourists.

CONTENTS

Translator's note: When preparing the recipes, follow the measurements either in metric or imperial; deciliters or cups (1 cup = 8 fluid ounces = 2 1/2 dl). Do not combine the two systems within one recipe.

Following pages: No domesticated animals have more freedom than Norwegian lambs. They spend their short hectic lives feeding on the abundant grasses of the Norwegian countryside. The result is an excellent basis for all kinds of lamb dishes.

FOREWORD

Cookbooks are one of the pleasures of life. They are found in vast numbers, with different themes and for all kinds of ingredients. They deal with fish and meat, berries and vegetables, mushrooms and pasta, cakes and desserts, describing dishes and culinary traditions from all over the world. There is no such thing as too many cookbooks. In this book, 35 leading Norwegian chefs present a variety of specialties from their restaurants. The recipes are based on Norwegian ingredients and may be considered Scandinavian in origin, but they have been inspired by trends from abroad. Some of the chefs included here are the best in Norway – many have won top prizes in major international competitions. Others are worthy representatives of the Norwegian hotel restaurant kitchen. All have been chosen as part of a culinary journey through Norway. It begins in the remote northeastern part of the country, on the Norwegian-Russian border, and continues along the coast of Finnmark southward toward Kristiansand, before it ends in the capital, Oslo.

For the most part, this book features recipes for festive occasions. Even though they originated in restaurant kitchens, they are not too complicated for home use. But, let it be said right from the start – most of these dishes were not created for dieters. This tends to be the case when top-class chefs are asked to present their very best. Each chef was given a list of ingredients and asked to create recipes to ensure variation in the choice of raw materials. Although the resulting recipes may not necessarily reflect the specialties of the featured restaurants, the ingredients will have been given a local flavor by the chef and his kitchen.

All recipes in this book have been adapted for the home kitchen, with ingredients readily available at the

supermarket. You do not have to be a master chef to prepare these dishes, but after your family and friends have enjoyed some of them, they will consider you far more accomplished than the average hobby cook.

There are no recipes for traditional Norwegian dishes, such as *lutefisk*, Bergen-style *raspeball* or *smalahuvud*. Nor is there any mention of *rømmegrøt* or *gammelost*. These dishes are all deeply rooted in the Norwegian traditional kitchen, but they can be an acquired taste. They can hardly be considered potential menu selections for cooks outside of Norway, an important audience for this book, or even for most Norwegians. It takes an appreciation for tradition as well as a little experience to be enthusiastic about such unusual Norwegian delicacies.

My heartfelt thanks to the Gastronomic Institute and Morten Schakenda for inspired collaboration. The Institute helped to select chefs and ingredients, and they also adapted the recipes. In addition, I would like to thank Harald Osa, former head of the Gastronomic Institute and current chef de cuisine at *Hotel Continental* in Oslo for his invaluable advice, and photographer Bengt Wilson, for his outstanding photographs. The translator of this book Melody Favish, contributed valuable advice regarding the adaptation of many recipes for the home kitchen. The Norwegian version benefited from this as well. We hope that the 95 recipes in the book will provide culinary inspiration as well as proof that Norwegian cuisine has improved considerably over the last decade or two. If the book makes the reader hungry and the guests of the house happy, then its goal has been achieved. Good food is meant to be shared with friends and family. *Bon appetit* and enjoy the trip.

Gunnar Jerman

From Nature's Pantry

Food is an important cultural medium, and it tells a great deal about a country's individual characteristics and identity. Culinary traditions reflect lifestyles as well as social and economic conditions through the ages. A nation's kitchen reveals what was cultivated and hunted in certain areas, how people lived, and methods of food preservation. Originally, availability, both at home and in restaurants, was governed by the seasons. Until relatively recently, the Norwegian ice cream season started on Constitution Day, May 17, and ended in the middle of August, on the last day of summer vacation. Salmon first appeared on the table in May and disappeared, along with strawberries, when the season ended in the fall. Specific ingredients have long been traditional geographical and seasonal markers in the Norwegian kitchen. Summer mackerel dishes on the west coast, the use of game in the central regions, local specialties such as Bergen fish soup, and Lofoten cod tongues are just a few examples.

The advent of the deep freezer revolutionized domestic households and made seasonal ingredients available year-round. The world has grown smaller, and affluent societies are no longer as dependent upon local and seasonal supplies as they were in the past. Different foods are always in season somewhere on the planet, and distance is no longer an obstacle. Even expensive air freight and refrigeration systems do not make foreign berries, fruit, and vegetables too expensive for the average consumer.

Far left: Salmon fishing made Norwegian rivers famous. Today, fishing at sea provides larger catches and can be practiced year-round. This mature cod or "skrei" from Senja illustrates why sports fishing at sea has become so popular.

The cod fisheries in the Lofoten Islands provided the basis for the first export of Norwegian fish to the growing cities of Europe almost 1000 years ago. The fish is dried in the cold breezes of northern Norway, just as was done in the Middle Ages, before it is shipped to markets around the world. This picture is from Hamnøy in Lofoten.

But culinary traditions linger on. No salmon tastes better than the first wild salmon caught in the spring, and no imported crayfish can compare with those harvested from Norwegian waters when the protected period draws to a close in August. And there are still those who splurge on a lobster feast when the traps are retrieved in October. Autumn is the season for lamb. Roast lamb and mutton and cabbage stew appear on the table when the sheep are brought home from their summer pastures. This coincides with the fall hunting season, which brings hearty game dishes steaming with the fragrance of the forests and mountains.

Even though modern preservation techniques have created new possibilities and markets for Norwegian products, there is still no substitute for fresh seafood. No amount of preparation can conjure up the taste and consistency of fresh fish. That is why displays of fresh fish are always so attractive and eye-catching anywhere in the world.

Norway is in a unique position as a food supplier. That food is produced in Arctic regions is considered both exotic and spectacular by foreigner consumers. At the same time, they know that the products come from clean waters. Conditions for growth along the long Norwegian coast are favorable, and Norway has been an important supplier of fish to cities in Europe and abroad for almost 1000 years. Tourist brochures describe northern Norway as Europe's last wilderness. The open seas of the north Atlantic are less polluted than more central bodies of water close to heavily industrialized areas and population centers. That, along with the cold, fresh depths along the Norwegian coast, establishes the basis for Norway's position as one of the world's largest exporter of seafood. With more attention focused on cleanliness and freshness, Norway has a competitive advantage, which it plans to maintain and further develop. Seafood is becoming an increasingly important part of a healthy diet. Even fish fat is healthy, as it can help to reduce cholesterol levels.

Never before has the fishing industry brought so much revenue to Norway. Even in an era when many other Norwegian specialties and delicacies have found international markets, fish and fish products remain our second largest export, second only to oil and gas. Ninety per cent of all fish caught by Norwegian vessels is exported, and people all over the world eat Norwegian fish. Continental Europe is still the most important market for Norwegian fish products, but Norwegian bacalao is known as far away as Brazil, and stockfish from Norway is sold at Nigerian markets. The fish-loving Japanese are loyal customers in the Far East.

An autumn day along a country road as the sheep are brought home from their mountain grazing pastures.

The earliest records of Norwegian foreign trade mention products from the far north, such as whale oil, furs, and fish. These exports made the north the richest part of Norway. As early as the 12th century, the migration of the cod to their spawning grounds off the coast of the Lofoten Islands provided the basis for Norway's largest seasonal fishery. For centuries, fish have been dried in the frigid Lofoten air, then sent south to Bergen to be exported to the growing cities of Europe. Fish from the north helped to make Bergen Norway's richest city and its medieval capital, one of the largest northern European cities in its heyday.

Later, other coastal fisheries came to play almost as great a role. Winter and spring herring fisheries became extremely important. The mighty cod dominated Norwegian fish exports through the 1970s, when a burgeoning aquaculture industry gradually brought salmon into the lead. The warm currents of the Gulf Stream keep the waters off the coast of Norway at a stable temperature throughout the year. Islands, holms, and skerries shield the coast from the seas beyond and create ideal conditions for the fish farms that have sprouted up along the Norwegian coast during the past 20 years. Today, more than half of all Atlantic farmed salmon comes from Norway. Thanks to Norwegian aquaculture technology, salmon is now available at reasonable prices worldwide.

High-quality Norwegian ingredients are not limited to seafood. Many kinds of game can be found in our forests and mountains, and the sound of sheep bells in fields and summer pastures bears witness to the significance of these woolly flocks in many districts. Norwegian sheep lead a happy, carefree life, short and intense though it may be. They are allowed to wander freely, with plenty of food, from birth in the spring until their short lives end in the fall. The result is some of the best lamb in the world.

It is common knowledge that the best berries are grown in cold climates. It is a wonder that many plants manage to grow at all as far north as Norway. Berries grow more slowly in the cold northern climate than in the south. That, combined with long summer days, produces fruit and vegetables with an unusually intense flavor, unequaled by the fast-growing products of warmer southern soil.

Today, traditional dishes are often influenced by international flavors and seasonings. Now more than ever before, people are traveling abroad and coming into contact with the modern international kitchen. This, along with newspapers, magazines, and television, has an effect on day-to-day food preparation. Restaurants have added an exciting new dimension to traditional dishes. Pizza and pasta have become commonplace in Norwegian homes and have added color and variety to the Norwegian diet. Ready-to-serve and semi-prepared foods have appeared on the dinner table in many homes for quite a while, partially as a result of the growing number of women in the workplace. Their lack of time for food preparation was quickly addressed by the food industry. Pre-cooked food is more popular than ever before.

These industrial products will retain their position in the future, but there is more interest in food than ever before. We appear to be on the threshold of a renaissance in the home kitchen as well. There has been an increase in the number of television programs and newspaper and magazine articles about food. All of this has an impact on what ends up on the dinner table. People are more health conscious than ever before and are therefore willing to pay more for high-quality ingredients. At the same time, they want to recapture the charm of dishes made by their mothers, and their mothers' mothers, but adapted to suit their new eating habits. They want to taste the ingredients, not disguise them.

As new food traditions emerge, Norway is looking to the future. The Norwegian kitchen has always focused on fresh fish, and the vast, easily available resources have led to an increase in fish-based products. In a world where the consumer is more conscious than ever of the effect of the environment on health and society, cleanliness is important. Many people lack clean air, clean water, and unpolluted nature. Thus it is even more important to use healthy ingredients, for ingredients determine the quality of a meal. Norway has an abundance of high-quality raw materials from the sea, the forest, and the mountains, ready to be sustainably harvested from nature's pantry.

740 fish farms are located along Norway's coast, as far north as Finnmark. In 1997, they produced 310,000 tons of Salmon. That is approximately 70 per cent of the total production of Atlantic farmed salmon.

The Arrival of the Gourmet

The first tourists who came to Norway were British adventurers seeking exotic experiences in the country's rugged landscape. They returned home with colorful descriptions of fjords and mountains, glaciers and waterfalls. They were not, however, impressed with the spartan accommodations or the food, even at a time when most mountain climbers would have been satisfied with basic food and shelter.

Just over a hundred years ago, tourist traffic began to increase. The simple lodgings provided by farms and inns were no longer sufficient to deal with the ever increasing flow of visitors, and they did not meet the growing demand for new comforts. The result was a period of hectic building activity. Old inns were expanded and new wooden hotels were built. Many hotels that opened at the turn of the century are now treasured as examples of outstanding Norwegian wooden architecture, which had its golden age during the *Belle Époque*.

It took a longer time for the Norwegian restaurant kitchen to reach an international level, which has only been achieved over the past 30 years. Before that, there were few exceptions to the heavy, staid, Norwegian country cooking that dominated the menus. Today, young chefs have taken over and have begun to prepare lighter and more elegant food. This development is not unique to Norway. Innovative French chefs led the way, and traces of French influence can be found in most up-scale Norwegian restaurants. Norwegian chefs traveled to France and set an enthusiastic example for young, ambitious disciples. Modern chefs are not confined to the kitchen, but are accountable and accessible outside the kitchen as never before. They perform for their public and many have gained celebrity status through television and other media. They have elevated their craft to art at the highest level and have generated a new sense of pride throughout the profession.

Foreign chefs taught the Norwegians to eat some of the more unusual types of fish. With its huge threatening jaws, the monkfish is no beauty, but it certainly is delicious.

Many of today's finest chefs have trained with these three masters. From the left, Hroar Dege, Willy Wyssenbach and Edgar Ludl. Each has made an important contribution to the emergence of the Norwegian restaurant kitchen.

It is difficult to pinpoint exactly when the new Norwegian kitchen became established. It did not sweep through the country quickly, nor did it reach all parts simultaneously. It has taken many years to reach the outlying districts. Strong personalities and important events were essential to its development. The breakthrough of the Norwegian cruise industry in the Caribbean at the end of the 1960s brought many foreign chefs into contact with Norway. They brought their own eating habits and specialties into cruise ship dining rooms. While onboard, they met Norwegian women. Cupid played his role, and after their contracts at sea ended, the chefs followed their female companions back to Norway. They stepped into key positions in several restaurants and exerted their influence both in and around Oslo. Eventually, they became more Norwegian than the Norwegians.

It was these foreign chefs who introduced their Norwegian colleagues to new and unusual ingredients. Many wonderful species of fish were labeled "trash fish" and were tossed back into the sea. Although these fish are considered good eating on Norwegian tables today, we must not forget that it took foreigners to teach Norwegians to use them. These "trash fish" were not beautiful. No ocean catfish, gray gurnard, or monkfish would ever win a beauty contest. But as far as flavor is concerned, they win hands down.

Even in Norway, there were chefs who began to open the eyes of their restaurant guests to new experiences. Three have been particularly influential – Willy Wyssenbach, originally from Switzerland, who became chef de cuisine at *Hotel Continental* in 1963, Norwegian Hroar Dege, who founded *Tre Kokker* in 1965, and Edgar Ludl of *Park Hotell*, Sandefjord, later of *Ludl's Gourmet*. Together, they can be considered the fathers of modern Norwegian cuisine. They inspired a new generation of chefs who are responsible for some of the best food in Norway today.

It is impossible to ignore the above trio when chronicling the development of Norwegian cuisine. They were pioneers, and it is largely due to their efforts that the profession of chef has risen in status and attracts so many young talents today. Wyssenbach, Dege, and Ludl created media interest in cooking and restaurants. Newspapers began to feature food and restaurant columns and television produced cooking shows. It has been a long time since training as a chef was among the least popular educational programs in the country. Now there are more applicants than ever before, and recruitment bodes well for further development of the Norwegian restaurant and hotel kitchen.

Oslo's *Hotel Continental* is in many ways unique. For a lifetime, Ellen Brochmann has run this family-owned hotel with a steady hand, refusing to compromise quality no matter what the cost. She was her own master, with no financial advisers and no stockholders to consider, and thus she could afford to follow her own principles. She made certain that top French chefs were brought in to develop the hotel kitchen, making

The members of this national culinary team will defend Norway's position in international competitions until the year 2000. In much the same way as world-class athletes, these competitors have to endure difficult training sessions and meets. From the left, Terje Ness, Charles Tjessem, Tom Viktor Gausdal, Morten Schakenda, Lars Barmen, Espen Vesterdal Larsen, Odd Ivar Solvold (team leader), Harald Osa (captain), Jørn Lie.

A Norwegian world champion is worthy of celebration no matter what his field. A jubilant Bent Stiansen, owner and manager of Statholdergaarden *in Oslo, won the prestigious* Bocuse d'Or *competition in Lyon in 1993.*

the *Continental* an institution with a great impact on the development of the Norwegian restaurant kitchen.

Hroar Dege introduced new, lighter French dishes. And it did not go unnoticed when he opened up his kitchen and brought the chefs into the restaurant. At the same time, Dege praised the quality of Norwegian ingredients and noted that the climate and landscape were ideal for producing the best products for the kitchen. The new emphasis was on retaining the original flavor of the ingredients, whether they were fish, meat, or berries. Hroar Dege was, and is, a rare species in the Norwegian landscape. His personality is engaging and his love of food is contagious. In those early days, he praised Norwegian food traditions and wrote persuasive books and articles stressing quality in every detail.

When Norway competed at the Culinary Olympics for the first time in 1980, only one member of the team was Norwegian, the rest were foreigners. That team, led by Edgar Ludl, had no sponsors or money. They prepared their dishes at their modest hotel. Their reward, a bronze medal, encouraged them to try again.

In the years since the first awkward attempts at competitions, the Norwegian Culinary Team has won praise and honor at large team events such as the American Classic and the Culinary Olympics. The Culinary Olympics are held every four years, with teams from over 30 nations. From 1895 to 1992, they were held in Frankfurt, but they were moved to Berlin in 1996. Over the past few years, Norway has soared up the ratings and must defend its second place from 1996 at the next Olympics in the year 2000. A new team led by Odd Ivar Solvold is already in training to defend this position, and they are sponsored by Norwegian industry. Sponsorship is just as important for Olympic chefs as it is for Olympic athletes.

On an individual basis, Norwegian chefs have done well in international competitions such as *Bocuse d'Or* in Lyon. The competition, which is held every other year, is considered the world championships for chefs. Bent Stiansen won it in 1993, Lars Erik Underthun won silver in 1991, and Odd Ivar Solvold won bronze in 1997. Today all three help to set the standard for ambitious and hard-working Norwegian chefs.

This book helps to illustrate that there are many good restaurants outside the major cities. Those presented in this book range from *Hotel Continental* and Oslo's *Michelin*-starred restaurants to informal eating places in towns and coastal villages. This range is due to the fact that many chefs return home after their education. Many have seen their dream of returning home and opening a restaurant come true. Although it will still be a while before the majority of Norwegian restaurants have achieved the level we would like, there is an ocean of difference between the standards of 30 years ago and today. We are really speaking about two different worlds. We can quote the *Michelin Guide* and say: The best are worth a journey, the next best are worth a detour.

Young chefs are like nomads, always moving around. They can take their talents and their recipes with them wherever they go. They settle down only when they open their own restaurants. We experienced this first-hand in this book. Many chefs have changed kitchens during the writing of this book, and others are sure to follow. But the restaurants presented here will remain, with new chefs who will do their best to maintain quality as well as add their own special touches.

Following pages: Winter in Reine in Lofoten.

Inger og Hans-Henrik Gunnermann:
PASVIK TAIGA, SKOGFOSS

Pasvik Taiga is located in the Pasvik Valley, in Norway's northeastern corner near the Russian border. It may be the only restaurant of its kind, right at the edge of the taiga, the huge forest which stretches all the way from the Bering Strait to Pasvik. The special wilderness menu is based on local fish and game. The Norwegian king and queen, as well as members of other European royal houses, have dined at *Pasvik Taiga*, and they have been impressed with both the food and the surroundings.

Inger (b. 1947) and Hans-Henrik Gunnermann (b. 1943 in Denmark) have created a gourmet restaurant in the remote border area of Skogfoss. Few others would have risked such a project. Everything about *Pasvik Taiga* is unusual – Inger and Hans-Henrik Gunnermann have added a new dimension to the Norwegian restaurant kitchen.

Russian or king crab came to Norwegian waters from the east. It is a giant among the creatures on the sea floor and can grow up to a meter and a half between its claws and weigh more than seven kilos (15 pounds). Pasvik Taiga features this exclusive delicacy on its menu. (See recipe pages 26-27).

MAIN COURSE
Baked Hare in Pastry
– Tundra Ecstasy

1 kg (2 1/4 lb) saddle of hare
350 g (12 oz) mushrooms, chopped
butter
rose peppercorns
fresh thyme
4 sheets (12 oz) puff pastry
8 thin slices cured ham, such as Parma ham
1 egg yolk
2 dl (3/4 cup) whipping cream
1 tsp cornstarch stirred into 2 tsp cold water

2 bananas
2 1/2 Tbsp orange liqueur
juice of 1 lemon
12 Brussels sprouts
orange slices
red currants

Cut the filets from the saddle of hare. Refrigerate.

Chop the bones and place in a saucepan just large enough to hold them in a single layer. Add water to cover (along with any vegetable trimmings). Cover and simmer 1 hour. Strain and reserve for sauce. There should be about 2 dl (3/4-1 cup). If there is more, reduce over high heat. Set aside.

Sauté the mushrooms in butter. Toward the end of the cooking time, add rose peppercorns and fresh thyme. Allow to cool.

Defrost the puff pastry and roll out on a lightly floured surface. Place a slice of ham on each, then a layer of mushrooms. Top with filet of hare, then more mushrooms and ham. Fold over and "seal" with egg yolk. Brush the top of each roll with egg yolk. Refrigerate one hour.

Preheat the oven (preferably a convection oven) to 225C (425F). Bake 14-15 minutes.

Meanwhile, reheat the stock and add the cream. Simmer a few minutes until thickened. If the sauce is still thin, stir in the cornstarch mixture and cook until thickened. Do not salt the sauce, as the ham is salty.

Halve one banana lengthwise and crosswise. Sauté until golden in orange liqueur. Slice the other banana and brush with lemon juice.

Clean and cook the Brussels sprouts in lightly salted water 2-3 minutes.

To serve, arrange the baked hare rolls on individual heated plates with bananas and Brussels sprouts. Spoon sauce all around. Garnish with orange slices, red currants and a sprig of thyme. 4 servings

DESSERT
Blueberries in Puff Pastry
– Blue Lust

2 sheets (6 oz) puff pastry
1 egg yolk
8 1/2 dl (3 1/2 cups) blueberries
4 Tbsp (1/4 cup) sugar

Ginger cream:
2 1/2 dl (1 cup) whipping cream
2 1/2 dl (1 cup) full-fat milk
3/4 dl (1/3 cup) sugar
3 egg yolks
1 Tbsp grated fresh ginger
1 Tbsp potato starch or cornstarch stirred into 1 Tbsp cold water

A few fresh blueberries or lemon balm leaves

Preheat the oven (preferably a convection oven) to 225C (425F). Defrost the puff pastry. Divide each sheet in two. With a sharp knife, cut a rectangle about 2 cm (3/4") from the edge in each, but do not cut all the way through. Brush with egg yolk. Bake 10-15 minutes.

Combine blueberries and sugar in a saucepan and heat until the sugar is dissolved.

Ginger cream: Scald cream and milk. Beat the sugar and egg yolks until light and lemon-colored. Whisk in the hot cream mixture. Stir in the ginger. Stir in the potato starch mixture and cook until thickened. Strain.

Remove the puff pastry lids. Fill the bases with warm ginger cream and blueberries. Garnish with fresh blueberries in season or lemon balm when fresh berries are not available. 4 servings

APPETIZER
Sautéed King Crab Glasnost

4 large king crab legs
olive oil

Stock:
crab shells
shrimp shells
1 garlic clove, chopped
olive oil
2 dl (3/4 cup) dry white wine or vermouth
1 1/2 dl (2/3 cup) mild chili sauce (ketchup-style)
1 dl (1/2 cup) whipping cream
tomato paste (optional)
chopped parsley and chives

lettuce leaves

Remove crab meat from shells and set aside.

Stock: Sauté the crab and shrimp shells with the garlic in a small amount of oil. Add the wine and reduce over high heat until about 3 Tbsp remain. Add water to cover and simmer about 30 minutes. Strain. Stir in the chili sauce. Bring to a boil and reduce by half, then add the cream and reduce again by about a half. Stir in a teaspoon or two of tomato paste for a brighter color and more pronounced tomato flavor, if desired. Add the chopped herbs.

Sauté the crabmeat in olive oil until golden.

Arrange lettuce on individual plates. Top with crabmeat and sauce. Garnish with fresh herbs. Serve with crusty bread.4 servings

Terje Larsen:
ALTASTUA, ALTA

As its name suggests, *Altastua* is located in Alta, the largest town in Finnmark, way above the Arctic Circle. An important commercial center for the western part of the region, Alta's main attractions are the prehistoric rock carvings at Hjemmeluft. 3000 carvings tell a story which dates back as far as 5000 BC. *Altastua* serves contemporary cuisine based on local ingredients. It is one of many excellent restaurants outside the major cities of southern Norway.

Terje Larsen (b. 1968) has a versatile background. He worked at *SAS* hotels in Bergen and Alta, at the *Conti Hansa Hotel* in Kiel, Germany, at the *North Cape Hall* and at the *North Cape Hotel* in Honningsvåg, before he came to Alta.

MAIN COURSE
Marinated Haddock

800 g (1 3/4 lb) boneless and skinless haddock fillet

3 garlic cloves, peeled
juice of 2 limes
50 g (1 3/4 oz) fresh ginger, sliced
3 dl (1 1/4 cups) olive oil
freshly ground white pepper

200 g (8 oz) fresh spinach
250 g (8 oz) broccoli
1 small cauliflower
4 carrots
1 leek

2 dl (3/4 cup) white wine
salt and pepper

3 shallots, minced
60 g (2 oz) butter
3 Tbsp whipping cream
1 Tbsp chopped parsley

Cut the fish into four pieces of equal size and place in double plastic bags.

Purée garlic, lime juice, ginger, all but one tablespoon of the oil and pepper to taste in a food processor one minute. Pour over the fish. Marinate in the refrigerator at least 4 hours, preferably overnight.

Preheat the oven to 200C (400F).Rinse the spinach well and remove any coarse stalks. Blanch in lightly salted boiling water for about 30 seconds. Divide the broccoli and cauliflower into florets. Blanch for one minute. Immediately plunge blanched vegetables into ice water. Drain, squeezing as much water as possible from the spinach. Peel and cut the carrot and leek into 4 cm (1 3/4") julienne. Place each piece of fish in the center of a sheet of aluminum foil. Top with vegetables. Spoon a little wine over each. Sprinkle with salt and pepper. Wrap the fish well, crimping the foil to seal. Bake 12-15 minutes.

Sauté shallots in remaining olive oil. Remove foil packets from the oven. Open carefully and pour any juices over the shallots. Simmer to reduce by a third. Remove from the heat and beat in the butter and cream. Garnish with parsley.

Serve fish, vegetables and sauce in deep plates with almond potatoes alongside. 4 servings

APPETIZER
Smoked Salmon with Scrambled Eggs and Herb Toast

300 g (10 oz) smoked salmon
1 beefsteak tomato
olive oil
salt and freshly ground pepper
1 garlic clove, minced
5 eggs
1 1/2 dl (2/3 cup) whipping cream
unsalted butter
1 Tbsp chopped herbs, such as dill, parsley and thyme
6 slices white bread
4 lettuce leaves

Cut the salmon into thin slices. Set aside.

Scald the tomato in boiling water for about 30 seconds, then peel, seed and quarter. Brush with oil and sprinkle with salt, pepper and garlic.

Whisk together eggs and cream. Season with salt and pepper. Melt butter in a frying pan and add the egg mixture. Cook over medium heat, stirring constantly, until lightly scrambled.

Melt butter in a large frying pan. Stir in the chopped herbs. Sauté the bread on both sides.

Divide the salmon and scrambled eggs among individual plates. Garnish with lettuce and tomato wedges. Halve the toast diagonally and serve alongside. 4 servings

MAIN COURSE
Reindeer Filet with Smoked Salmon

4 baking potatoes
olive oil
salt and pepper
2 Tbsp chopped oregano and/or thyme

640 g (1 1/2 lb) reindeer filet
100 g (4 oz) smoked salmon
4 thin slices bacon

200 g (8 oz) oyster or button mushrooms
2 red onions
5 dl (2 cups) whipping cream
2-3 Tbsp Cognac

2 carrots
1 rutabaga
butter

Preheat the oven to 225C (425F). Scrub the potatoes and cut into wedges. Combine 2 Tbsp oil with salt, pepper and chopped herbs in an oven tray. Add the potatoes, turning to coat evenly. Bake until crispy, about 20 minutes.

Divide the reindeer filet into four pieces of equal size and cut a lengthwise pocket in each. Cut the salmon into four strips and place one in each pocket. Wrap with bacon. Sauté in oil, about 3-4 minutes per side. Wrap the meat in aluminum foil and allow to rest 8-10 minutes before serving.

Clean and quarter the mushrooms and cut the onions into wedges. Sauté lightly in oil, then add Cognac and ignite. Add cream and simmer until reduced by about half.

Peel carrots and rutabaga and cut into batons. Steam in a small amount of water with a pat of butter for 3-4 minutes.

Spoon sauce onto individual plates. Cut each filet into thirds and place on the sauce. Arrange the vegetables all around. Serve with potatoes. 4 servings

Odd Pedersen:
ODDS MAT OG VINHUS, HAMMERFEST

Odds Mat og Vinhus (Odd's Food and Wine House) overlooks the harbor in Hammerfest, the northernmost town in the world. West Finnmark's leading restaurant is just six years old. The ambiance is cozy, with an open rotisserie behind a counter decorated with ships' rigging and sealskins. *Odds Mat og Vinhus* has received a number of awards, including best Norwegian food on a restaurant menu.

Odd Pedersen (b. 1950) is one of many chefs who trained at a maritime cook and steward school and apprenticed with the Norwegian Merchant Marines. He has also worked at *Park Hotell* in Sandefjord.

MAIN COURSE
Cod with Head, Liver and Roe

800 g (1 3/4 lb) skinless and boneless cod fillets
2 cod heads
2 cod roes
500 g (1 lb) cod liver

1 1/4 dl (1/2 cup) salt
2 liters (quarts) water

Rinse the fish and cut into four pieces of equal size. Split the heads. Halve the roe and pack in baking parchment or aluminum foil. Remove membrane from the liver and rinse well. Cut into cubes.

Bring salt and water to a boil. Place the roe in a saucepan and add boiling salted water to cover.

Simmer 30-40 minutes. Place the heads in another saucepan and add boiling salted water to cover. Simmer about 5 minutes. Skim, then add the fish fillets. Add more boiling salted water to cover. Simmer until the fish is firm and white, 6-7 minutes.

Cut the fish liver into bite-size pieces and place in a small saucepan. Cover with water. Do not add salt. Cook about 5 minutes. Add salt and cook 5 minutes more.

Serve the fish, heads and roe with buttered carrots and boiled potatoes. Serve the liver with finely chopped onion and flatbread on the side. 4 servings

APPETIZER
Marinated Game with Mustard Sauce and Creamed Spinach

200 g (8 oz) trimmed loin of hare or reindeer
10 juniper berries, crushed
1 Tbsp salt
1 Tbsp sugar
4 Tbsp (1/4 cup) gin

Creamed spinach:
100 g (4 oz) fresh spinach
1/2 dl (3 1/2 Tbsp) whipping cream
1 tsp flour stirred into 2 tsp whipping cream
salt and pepper

Mustard sauce:
2 Tbsp whipping cream
2 Tbsp mayonnaise
1 Tbsp sweet mustard
1 Tbsp chopped pickle
1 Tbsp chopped dill

lingonberries
orange sections

Place the meat in a glass baking dish. Sprinkle with crushed juniper berries, salt and sugar, and drizzle with gin. Cover with plastic wrap and marinate in the refrigerator for 48 hours. Just before serving, dry off the meat with paper towels and cut into thin slices.

Rinse the spinach well and remove any coarse stalks. Blanch in lightly salted boiling water for about 30 seconds. Immediately plunge into ice water. Drain, squeezing out as much water as possible, chop and return to the pan. Add the cream and simmer until thickened. If the sauce is too thin, stir in the flour mixture and cook until thickened. Season with salt and pepper.

Whisk together all ingredients for the mustard sauce.

Divide the creamed spinach among individual plates. Top with meat. Drizzle mustard sauce all around. Garnish with lingonberries and orange sections. Serve with thin slices of toast. 4 servings

Anders Blomkvist:
COMPAGNIET RESTAURATION, TROMSØ

Compagniet Restauration is a charming place. The food is exquisite, and there is a feeling of tradition and history in the old building constructed of Russian pine and larch logs in 1837. At that time, the house on *Sjøgata* (Sea Street) was both the office and home of a merchant named Dreyer. Many generations of merchants lived in the building before it became a restaurant.

Anders Blomkvist (b. 1960 in Sweden) trained and worked as a chef his homeland before coming to Norway. In 1990, he became part-owner and chef at *Compagniet*. He may not have the most extensive menu in Tromsø, but all his dishes bear the mark of a master.

APPETIZER
Shrimp-Filled Ham Rolls on Bitter Greens

200-300 g (8-10 oz) dried cured ham, in thin slices
3/4 dl (1/3 cup) minced red onion
200 g (8 oz) cooked shelled tiny shrimp
2-3 Tbsp crème fraîche or dairy sour cream
1 curly endive

Vinaigrette:
1 part lemon juice
3 parts oil
salt and pepper

Spread the slices of ham on a tray. Combine onion, shrimp and crème fraîche. Spoon onto the ham and roll up.

Wash the endive and spin dry. Arrange the leaves on a large dish. Top with the ham rolls. Whisk together lemon juice and oil. Season with salt and pepper and drizzle over the ham rolls. 4 servings

DESSERT
Warm Blackberry Soup with Port Wine and Vanilla Ice Cream

1 vanilla bean
1 liter (4 cups) blackberries
1 1/4 dl (1/2 cup) sugar
1 dl (1/3 cup) water
1 cinnamon stick
1 dl (1/3 cup) Port wine
1 tsp cocoa powder

vanilla ice cream or whipped cream.

Split the vanilla bean and scrape out the seeds. Reserve the bean itself for another use. Combine vanilla, berries, sugar and water in a saucepan and bring to a boil. Purée with an immersion blender, then sieve, discarding the pits. Return the mixture to the saucepan and add the cinnamon stick, half the wine and the cocoa. Heat, then add remaining wine. Remove the cinnamon stick before serving.

Serve with vanilla ice cream or whipped cream. 4 servings

A view of Tromsø framed with Tromsø palms.

MAIN COURSE
Baked Pollack with Glazed Root Vegetables and Balsamic Juices

4 thick slices pollack (about 300 g (10 oz) each) with skin and
  bones
salt and pepper

1 medium carrot
1/4 medium rutabaga
1 chunk celeriac
4 medium shallots
10 cm (4") thick leek
3 dl (1 1/4 cups) chicken stock

4 Tbsp (1/4 cup) olive oil
250 g (8 oz) unsalted butter
1 Tbsp sugar
4 Tbsp (1/4 cup) balsamic vinegar

Preheat the oven to 200C (400F). Tie the fish into round tournedos. Sprinkle with salt and pepper. Place in a greased baking dish. Bake 10-15 minutes.

Clean the vegetables and cut into bite-sized pieces. Heat the chicken stock to boiling and add the vegetables. Blanch 2 minutes. Transfer to paper towels to drain.

Heat oil and 2 Tbsp of the butter in a frying pan. Add vegetables and sugar. Sauté until vegetables are coated. Season with salt and pepper.

Simmer the chicken stock until reduced by half. Add balsamic vinegar and reduce a few minutes more. Just before serving, whisk in the remaining butter and season with salt and pepper. Do not allow the sauce to boil.

Divide the vegetables among individual plates. Top with the fish. Ladle the juices all around. 4 servings

Jørn Kornør:
GRILLEN SAS HOTEL, TROMSØ

Tromsø residents and students alike appreciate good food and nights out on the town. That's why the choice of good restaurants is broader than one might ordinarily expect in a city this far north. Although hotel restaurants are not often among the most exciting, *Grillen Restaurant*, in the *Tromsø Radisson SAS Hotel*, is an exception, with grilled dishes and fish as its specialties.

Jørn Kornør (b. 1963) received his earliest training in the kitchen of a coastal steamer when he was 18. In addition to stints at the *SAS Royal Hotel* in Tromsø, he has made guest appearances at the well-known Swedish restaurants, *Stallmästaregården* and *Ulriksdals Wärdshus* in Stockholm. In January, 1994, he took over as chef at the *Radisson SAS Hotel* in Tromsø. Kornør was team captain for the apprentices who won the Nordic Championship in 1994.

Stockfish with tomatoes and shallots. Recipe on following page.

MAIN COURSE
Stockfish with Tomatoes and Shallots

800 g (1 3/4 lb) skinless and boneless stockfish (dried fish),
  pre-soaked
4 large tomatoes
6-7 shallots
olive oil
1 dl (scant 1/2 cup) fish stock
salt and pepper
250 g (8 oz) bacon
12 snow peas
butter

Cut the fish into serving pieces. Bring a large pot of salted water to a boil. Add the fish. Simmer about 20 minutes.

Scald the tomatoes in boiling water for about 30 seconds, then peel, seed and dice.

Peel and slice the shallots. Sauté in olive oil until tender. Fold in the tomatoes. Bring to a boil, add the stock and simmer until thickened. Season with salt and pepper.

Dice the bacon and fry in its own fat until crispy and golden. Clean the snow peas and steam in lightly salted water with a pat of butter.

Divide the shallots among individual plates. Top with the fish and sprinkle with bacon and snow peas.

Serve with boiled potatoes. 4 servings

MAIN COURSE
Sautéed Wolffish with Tomato-Herb Sauce

1 shallot, minced
2 Tbsp butter
1 dl (1/3 cup) white wine
5 dl (2 cups) fish stock
1/2 dl (3 1/2 Tbsp) whipping cream
2 tsp cornstarch stirred into 2 tsp cold water (optional)

800 g (1 3/4 lb) wolffish, also called ocean catfish
butter
1 Tbsp minced shallots
1 tsp chopped parsley
1 tsp chopped dill
1 tsp chopped chives
1 tsp chopped basil
1 Tbsp tomato paste

Sauté the shallot in butter. Add wine and reduce over high heat until about 2 Tbsp remain. Add fish stock and reduce until about 3 1/2 dl (1 1/2 cups) remain. Stir in the cream. If the sauce is too thin, stir in the cornstarch mixture and cook until thickened.

Cut the fish into four pieces of equal size. Sauté in butter on both sides over medium heat until golden. Season with salt and pepper. Remove from the pan and keep warm.

In the same pan, sauté shallot and herbs in butter. Stir in the tomato paste. Add the white wine sauce and bring to a boil. Season to taste.

Serve the fish with boiled potatoes, buttered vegetables and the white wine sauce. 4 servings

Espen Jørgensen:
DE 4 ROSER, HARSTAD

De 4 Roser (The Four Roses) opened in 1996 but has already succeeded in becoming the pride of Harstad. The open Italian/French-inspired kitchen has been adapted to the North-Norwegian temperament and provides an intimate and cozy setting for a fine meal. *De 4 Roser* is another example of a excellent restaurant outside the larger towns of southern Norway.

Espen Jørgensen (b. 1970) received his chef's qualifications from the *Grand Nordic Hotel* in Harstad in 1991. After a few years of practice, including a stint at *Lofoten Fish Restaurant* at Aker Brygge in Oslo, he returned to his hometown, where he has made a name for himself at *De 4 Roser*.

APPETIZER
Salad with Sautéed Stockfish and Olives
in Herb Vinaigrette

1 fillet stockfish (dried fish)

Herb vinaigrette:
1/2 dl (3 1/2 Tbsp) wine vinegar
1 tsp Dijon mustard
1 tsp sugar
1/2 tsp salt
2 dl (3/4 cup) olive oil
1/2 dl (3 1/2 Tbsp) chopped fresh herbs

2 Tbsp olive oil
salt and pepper

4 large tomatoes, peeled and sliced
1 onion, thinly sliced
20 black pitted olives
chopped herbs

Soak the stockfish in cold water for 12-15 hours. Keep refrigerated.

Whisk together vinegar, mustard, sugar and salt. Whisk in the oil in a thin stream until emulsified. Stir in the chopped herbs. The vinaigrette should steep for at least two hours.

Dry the fish well. Pound with a meat mallet and tear into thin strips about 5 cm (2″) long. Heat a frying pan until almost smoking. Add 2 Tbsp olive oil. Stir-fry the fish for about 20 seconds. Drain on paper towels. Season with salt and pepper.

Place fish, tomatoes, onion and olives in a large bowl. Toss lightly with about 1 1/2 dl (2/3 cup) of the vinaigrette. Grind fresh black pepper over the salad and garnish with fresh herbs. Serve additional dressing alongside. 4 servings

MAIN COURSE
Baked Halibut with Early Cabbage and Tarragon Tomato Sauce

Sauce:
4 tomatoes
2 shallots, minced
1 garlic clove, minced
1/2 dl (3 1/2 Tbsp) olive oil
1 1/2 dl (2/3 cup) water
1 Tbsp tomato paste
2 Tbsp butter
2 Tbsp fresh tarragon leaves

800 g (1 3/4 lb) boneless
* halibut fillet, skin on*
salt and pepper

200 g (8 oz) celeriac
1 dl (scant 1/2 cup) whipping
* cream*

200 g (8 oz) early cabbage
3 Tbsp butter

fresh herbs

Scald the tomatoes in boiling water for about 30 seconds, then peel, seed and chop. Combine with shallots, garlic, oil, water and tomato paste in a saucepan and simmer over low heat about 30 minutes. Stir in butter and tarragon and keep warm. Do not allow to boil.

Preheat the oven to 225C (425F). Cut the fish into four pieces of equal size. Bake, skin side up, in a greased oven tray for about 8 minutes. Remove from the oven and carefully remove the skin. Season with salt and pepper.

Peel and cube the celeriac. Bring the cream slowly to a boil, then add the celeriac. Cover and simmer until tender. Transfer to a food processor and purée until smooth, about 15 seconds. Season with salt and pepper. Keep warm.

Cut the cabbage into 1 cm (1/2") slices and cook in lightly salted water until tender, about 2 minutes. Drain and stir in the butter. Season to taste.

Divide the sauce among individual heated plates. Place a mound of cabbage in the center. Top with fish and a large spoonful of celeriac purée. Garnish with fresh herbs.
4 servings

Following pages: Charming Henningsvær on a Sunday during Lofot fishing season.

Otto Asheim:
FISKEKROGEN, HENNINGSVÆR

Guests with window seats at *Restaurant Fiskekrogen* in Henningsvær in the Lofoten Islands can watch fishing boats come and go as they enjoy their meal. The protected harbor near Lofoten's fishing banks has made quaint little Henningsvær one of Norway's most important fishing villages. During the winter, fishermen come to Henningsvær from all around the area to harvest mature cod, called *skrei* in Norwegian, which swim into the Barents Sea to spawn.

Else-Marie Larsen from Lofoten and Otto Asheim from Trondheim met at hotel and catering college. They decided to settle in Lofoten and opened *Fiskekrogen* in 1989. Otto Asheim (b. 1952) has always been in charge of the kitchen. Many were skeptical about the idea of a fish restaurant in Henningsvær, but over the years, *Fiskekrogen* has won many hearts in Norway and abroad. The guest book tells of both local and foreign guests, from neighbors and ordinary tourists to royalty.

MAIN COURSE
Fish Cakes with Vegetables and Tartar Sauce

900 g (2 lb) skinless and
  boneless haddock fillets
4 tsp salt
4 Tbsp (1/4 cup) potato
starch
4 Tbsp (1/4 cup) chopped
  onion
1 dl (scant 1/2 cup) half
  and half or light cream
2 tsp nutmeg
100 g (4 oz) skinless and
  boneless salmon fillet

1 small zucchini
1 large red onion
2 medium carrots
2 1/2 Tbsp butter
1 1/2 dl (2/3 cup) white wine vinegar
2 tsp sugar
1 tsp salt

Tartar sauce:
2 dl (3/4 cup) mayonnaise
2 Tbsp chopped pickles
2 Tbsp chopped parsley
1 Tbsp capers
4 tsp chopped anchovies
2 Tbsp chopped onion
3 Tbsp whipping cream
3 Tbsp pickle brine

Grind the haddock once through a meat grinder with the coarsest disc, or pulse in a food processor until coarsely chopped. Add salt, potato starch, onion and nutmeg. With the motor running, gradually add the half and half. Transfer to a bowl. Cut the salmon into 1 cm (1/2") dice and fold into the fish purée. Refrigerate until ready to fry.

Clean and julienne the vegetables. Sauté in butter over medium heat about 5 minutes. Add vinegar, sugar and salt and cook carefully 5 minutes more.

Tartar sauce: Combine mayonnaise, pickles, parsley, capers, anchovies and onion. Thin with cream and pickle brine.

Form eight patties of the fish mixture. Fry in butter on both sides until golden.

Serve the fish cakes with glazed vegetables and potatoes fried in butter. Serve the tartar sauce alongside. 4 servings

APPETIZER

Seafood Mousse with Ocean Crayfish and Herb Sauce

40 g (1 1/2 oz) bladder wrack
  (seaweed) or spinach
4 dl (1 2/3 cups) fish stock
3 Tbsp aspic powder or gelatin
2 1/2 dl (1 cup) whipping
  cream
1 1/4 dl (1/2 cup) cooked
  shelled tiny shrimp
1 1/4 dl (1/2 cup) cooked
  shelled mussels
3 Tbsp salmon caviar
1/4 tsp freshly ground white
  pepper
1 1/2 dl (2/3 cup) mayonnaise
juice of 1 lemon
salt

Herb sauce:
2 Tbsp chopped fresh dill
2 Tbsp chopped fresh
  tarragon
2 Tbsp chopped fresh basil
2 Tbsp chopped fresh chervil
1 dl (1/2 cup) crème fraîche
1 tsp garlic pepper
2 Tbsp white wine vinegar
1 dl (1/3 cup) mayonnaise
1/2 tsp salt

8 ocean crayfish

fresh dill
lemon wedges

Clean the seaweed and blanch in lightly salted boiling water for about 2 minutes (spinach for about 30 seconds). Drain, then plunge immediately into cold water. Finely chop or purée in a food processor. Bring the fish stock to a boil. Remove from the heat and stir in the aspic powder. Chill until the aspic thickens slightly. Whip the cream. Fold in the seafood and seasonings. Combine fish aspic and mayonnaise and fold carefully into the seafood cream. Season to taste with lemon juice and salt. Spoon into a 2 liter (quart) mold. Refrigerate until set, at least 2 hours.

Herb sauce: Purée the first seven ingredients in a food processor. Fold in the mayonnaise and salt. Store in the refrigerator.

Bring lightly salted water to a boil. Remove from the heat. Add the crayfish and steep for one minute. Remove the crayfish and allow to cool for one minute. Halve lengthwise and remove the black vein.

Arrange two crayfish with a slice of mousse on each plate. Spoon sauce all around. Serve remaining sauce alongside. Garnish with fresh dill and lemon wedges. Serve with bread. 4 servings

MAIN COURSE

Sautéed Redfish with Root Vegetables and Cured Ham

700 g (1 3/4 lb) boneless and skinless redfish fillets

1/4 medium celeriac
1/4 medium rutabaga
1 medium red onion
1/4 large zucchini
1 medium beet
1/4 small leek
2 dl (3/4 cup) water
3 dl (1 1/4 cups) crème fraîche
2 tsp chopped fresh chervil
2 tsp chopped fresh basil
salt and freshly ground white pepper

3 Tbsp soy sauce
1 1/4 dl (1/2 cup) flour
olive oil

4 slices cured ham
lemon wedges
fresh basil

Cut the fish into eight serving pieces, two per person.

Clean and peel the vegetables. Cut into 1 1/2 cm (3/4″) dice. There should be about the same amount of each vegetable except for the leek, which should measure about half that amount. Simmer in lightly salted water until tender, about 5 minutes. Add the crème fraîche and bring to a boil. Stir in herbs and season with salt and pepper.

Sprinkle the fish with soy sauce and pepper. Dip in flour and fry in oil on both sides until golden brown, about 4 minutes.

Divide the creamed vegetables among individual plates. Top each with two pieces of fish. Roll up each ham slice and place on the fish. Garnish with lemon wedges and fresh basil. Serve with boiled almond potatoes. 4 servings

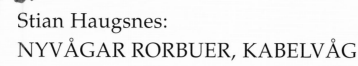

Stian Haugsnes:
NYVÅGAR RORBUER, KABELVÅG

Nyvågar Rorbuhotell in Storvågan in the Lofoten Islands is another destination worth a visit. Storvågan became a center for the cod-fishing industry almost 1000 years ago. Thanks to seasonal fishing, Lofoten thrived. During the last century, there were 90 fishermen's cottages, called *rorbuer* in Norwegian, in Storvågan. As many as 2000 fishermen lived here during cod-fishing season. Today, this historic settlement is a cultural and tourist center with a museum, an aquarium, an art gallery and *Nyvågar Rorbuhotell*. The hotel restaurant, *Lorchstua*, is named after Caspar Fredrik Lorch, the local landlord, who settled in Storvågan in 1811. He constructed the building which houses the Lofot Museum today.

Stian Haugsnes (b. 1973) is from Henningsvær. He studied in Lofoten, and won the Norwegian and Nordic Championships for apprentices in 1994. He is in a perfect position to utilize all the fantastic local fish, including the mighty cod, on his menus.

MAIN COURSE
Pollack with Bay Scallops in White Wine Sauce

10 bay scallops
2 lemons
1 Tbsp chopped fresh thyme
1 Tbsp chopped fresh parsley

2 carrots
1 small leek
1 black salsify
1 small celeriac

2 Tbsp minced onion
1 Tbsp clarified butter or vegetable oil
3 dl (1 1/4 cups) white wine
5 dl (2 cups) rich fish stock
3 dl (1 1/4 cups) whipping cream
salt and pepper

700 g (1 1/2 lb) boneless and skinless pollack fillet

Halve the scallops horizontally and place in a bowl. Squeeze the lemons over and fold in the fresh herbs. Marinate until needed.

Clean and peel the vegetables. Cut into chunks. Cook each separately in a small amount of lightly salted water until tender. Keep warm. Or, cook in advance until almost tender, then plunge in cold water. Reheat just before serving.

Sauté the onion in butter or oil until transparent. Add white wine and reduce over high heat until about 1 dl (1/3 cup) remains. Add fish stock and reduce by half. Add the cream and reduce to about 3 dl (1 1/4 cups). Strain. Season with salt and pepper. Keep warm.

Preheat the oven to 200C (400F). Cut the fish into four pieces of equal size. Make small slits and insert the marinated scallops. Place in an ovenproof dish and bake about 10-15 minutes.

Divide the vegetables among individual plates. Top with the fish. Ladle the sauce all around. Serve with boiled potatoes. 4 servings

MAIN COURSE
Wolffish-Shellfish Fricassee

700 g (1 1/2 lb) boneless and skinless wolffish (also called ocean catfish) fillets
2 carrots
1 leek
1 small celeriac
1 small bunch broccoli
1 liter (quart) rich fish stock
2 dl (3/4 cup) whipping cream
1 Tbsp cornstarch stirred into 1 Tbsp cold water
2 Tbsp chopped parsley
1 dl (scant 1/2 cup) crème fraîche (or whipping cream)
salt and pepper
2 1/2 dl (1 cup) cooked shelled shrimp
2 1/2 dl (1 cup) cooked shelled mussels

Cut the fish into four pieces of equal size. Clean and peel the vegetables. Cut into chunks. Cook each separately in fish stock until tender. Set aside and keep warm.

Simmer the fish in the stock for about 5 minutes. Remove and keep warm. Stir the cream into the stock and simmer for about 5 minutes. Stir in the cornstarch mixture and cook until thickened. Stir in parsley and crème fraîche. Season to taste with salt and pepper. Return fish and vegetables to the sauce. Add shrimp and mussels. Heat through but do not allow to boil. Serve in soup bowls with boiled potatoes alongside. 4 servings

Trond O. Kolstad:
BRYGGEN RESTAURANT, TRONDHEIM

Bryggen Restaurant is part of the 200-year-old wharf near the old city bridge in Bakklandet in Trondheim, with a view of the river and the cathedral. The gourmet restaurant, furnished in a rustic romantic style, with blue walls and white lace curtains, was opened in 1983. "Good food is even better with good service" is *Bryggen's* motto.

Trond Olav Kolstad (b. 1964) has trained and worked exclusively in Trondheim. He apprenticed at *Krovertens Hus* and worked for nearly seven years at the *Royal Garden* and *Grand Olav* hotels before he took over *Bryggen* in partnership with Abdul Basit.

APPETIZER
Clear Fish Soup with Smoked Salmon

Fish stock:
1 kg (2 1/4 lb) salmon bones and trimmings, rinsed
2 liters (quarts) cold water
1 medium carrot, in chunks
1 medium onion, sliced
1/2 medium leek, sliced
2 bay leaves
10 white peppercorns

20 mussels
1 dl (1/2 cup) white wine
2 Tbsp chopped onion

olive oil
20 small, thin slices smoked salmon
1 small zucchini
1 medium carrot, julienned
2 Tbsp minced onion
10 spinach leaves, shredded
salt and pepper
4 Tbsp (1/4 cup) chopped chives

Fish stock: Place all ingredients in a soup pot and bring to a boil. Skim well. Lower heat and simmer slowly for about 45 minutes. Strain. There should be about 8 dl (3 1/3 cups). If there is more, reduce to the required amount.

Place mussels, wine and onion in a saucepan. Steam over medium heat until shells open, about 5 minutes. Remove from heat and remove mussels from shells. Set aside.

Brush four soup bowls with oil. Line with salmon slices so that the edge is even around the entire bowl.

Cut the zucchini into 4 3-cm (1 1/4") lengths. Cut into a pretty shape with a knife. Save the trimmings. Hollow out the squash and blanch with the carrot in lightly salted water about 1 minute. Julienne any remaining zucchini.

Sauté the mussels in a small amount of oil with the onion and spinach. Season with salt and pepper.

Place the warm squash in the center of the salmon. Spoon vegetables all around. Top with the mussels. Ladle over the hot soup. Sprinkle with chopped chives. 4 servings

DESSERT
Mascarpone Passion Fruit Mousse

Base:
5 egg whites
3 dl (1 1/4 cups) confectioner's sugar
4 Tbsp (1/4 cup) sugar
1 1/4 dl (1/2 cup) finely ground almonds
1 1/2 dl (2/3 cup) finely ground hazelnuts
2 Tbsp finely ground walnuts or a total of about 3 dl
  (1 1/4 cups) finely ground mixed nuts

Mousse:
1 1/4 dl (1/2 cup) cottage cheese
1 1/2 dl (2/3 cup) mascarpone
1 1/2 dl (2/3 cup) sugar
5 sheets (tsp powdered) gelatin
1 1/4 dl (1/2 cup) passion fruit juice
3 1/4 dl (1 1/3 cups) whipping cream

Cocoa Sorbet:
4 dl (1 2/3 cups) water
1 dl (scant 1/2 cup) milk
1 3/4 dl (3/4 cup) sugar
2 Tbsp glucose
3/4 dl (1/3 cup) cocoa
120 g (4 oz) semi-sweet chocolate

Poached Apricots:
12 fresh apricots
1/2 vanilla bean
5 dl (2 cups) water
2 dl (3/4 cup) sugar
pinch saffron

Raspberry Sauce:
4 dl (1 3/4 cups) frozen raspberries
confectioner's sugar
lemon juice

lemon balm or mint leaves

Base: Preheat the oven to 180C (350F). Beat the egg whites with half the sugar for 3 minutes. Add remaining sugar and beat to a stiff meringue. Fold in the nuts. Line a baking sheet with baking parchment and spread the mixture over the sheet in a 1 cm (1/2 ") layer. Bake until

crispy on the edges and "chewy" in the center, about 15 minutes. Allow to cool. Using a 6 cm (2 1/4 ") round cookie cutter, cut out as many discs as possible.

Form rings with bands of aluminum foil, four layers thick, 6 cm (2 1/4") in diameter and 4 cm (1 3/4") high. Fasten with paper clips.

Mousse: Place both cheeses and sugar in the bowl of a food processor and process until smooth. Transfer to a bowl. Soak the gelatin sheets in (sprinkle the powdered gelatin over 1 Tbsp) cold water to soften, about 5 minutes. Squeeze excess water from gelatin sheets (disregard for powdered gelatin) and melt the softened gelatin in a small amount of the passion fruit juice. Combine with remaining juice and stir into the cheese mixture. Whip the cream and fold into the cheese mixture.

Place the cake bases in the foil forms and fill with mousse. Refrigerate, preferably overnight.

Sorbet: Bring water, milk, sugar, glucose and cocoa to a boil. Lower heat and simmer 10 minutes. Break the chocolate into small pieces and add. Stir until melted. Allow to cool. Freeze in an ice cream machine or in the freezer. If using the latter method, transfer to a food processor just before serving and pulse until semi-soft.

Apricots: Halve the apricots and remove the pit. Cut into wedges. Split the vanilla bean lengthwise and place in a saucepan with water, sugar, saffron and apricots. Bring to a boil, lower heat and poach the apricots until tender, 10-15 minutes. Allow to cool.

Sauce: Defrost the berries and purée 10 seconds in a food processor. Strain. Add confectioner's sugar and lemon juice to taste.

To serve, remove the mousse cakes from the forms and place on individual plates. Spoon the apricots all around. Top the mousse with scoops of sorbet and drizzle sauce all around. Garnish with lemon balm or mint leaves.

MAIN COURSE
Redfish Fricassee

Sauce:
5 dl (2 cups) whipping cream
3 Tbsp crème fraîche
1 1/2 tsp salt
1/2 tsp ground white pepper
1/2 tsp minced fresh ginger
juice of 1/2 lemon

100 g (4 oz) snow peas,
  coarsely chopped
2 stalks celery, coarsely
  chopped
1 medium parsnip, coarsely
  chopped
5 scallions, sliced diagonally
1 medium red onion, in wedges
1/2 medium onion, chopped

16 small almond potatoes
1 dl (1/2 cup) white wine
5 Tbsp (1/3 cup) minced onion
1/2 Tbsp caraway seeds

8 boneless redfish (or snapper)
  fillets, 4 with skin and
  4 skinless
flour
salt and pepper
olive oil

4 Tbsp (1/4 cup) chopped
  onion
3 Tbsp white wine
1 medium tomato, scalded,
  peeled, seeded and cut into
  wedges
4 Tbsp (1/4 cup) chopped
  chives

Sauce: Reduce the cream over high heat until 3 dl
(1 1/4 cups) remain. Stir in the remaining ingredients.
Set aside.

Blanch the vegetables in lightly salted boiling water for
about one minute.

Boil the potatoes in water to cover with the wine, onion
and caraway seeds until tender.

Dip the skin-on fish fillets in seasoned flour, then fry in
oil on both sides. Keep warm. Steam the skinless fillets
about 4 minutes.

Sauté the blanched vegetables in 1 tsp olive oil with the
chopped onion. Add the wine and season with salt and
pepper. Add the vegetables to the sauce. Just before
serving, reheat and fold in the tomato and chives.

Arrange sauce and vegetables in the center of individual
plates. Top with fish and serve with almond potatoes
alongside. 4 servings

Mindor Klauset:
SJØBUA RESTAURANT, ÅLESUND

Restaurant Sjøbua, right on the water in Ålesund, is the place for seafood lovers. Inside, there are tanks with live lobsters and fish, so guests can be assured of the freshest and best ingredients the Møre coast has to offer.

Mindor Klauset (b. 1973) served his apprenticeship at *Restaurant Sjøbua*. He is still there, and despite his youth, he is now chef.

APPETIZER
Traditional Marinated Salmon with Mustard Sauce and Creamed Potatoes

DESSERT
Pears Poached in Lingonberries

500 g (1 1/4 lb) skinless and boneless salmon fillet
1 Tbsp salt
1 1/2 Tbsp sugar
1 dl (1/2 cup) chopped dill pepper
2 Tbsp Cognac

Mustard sauce:
4 Tbsp (1/4 cup) coarse grain mustard
1 Tbsp sugar
2 Tbsp vinegar
2 egg yolks
2 dl (3/4 cup) vegetable oil
salt and pepper

Creamed potatoes:
2 Tbsp chopped onion
2 Tbsp butter
4 Tbsp (1/4 cup) flour
2 1/2 dl (1 cup) full-fat milk
2 1/2 dl (1 cup) whipping cream
8 boiled potatoes, cubed
chopped dill

3 dl (1 1/4 cups) water
2 dl (3/4 cup) lingonberries
1 3/4 dl (3/4 cup) sugar
1/2 cinnamon stick
1 tsp whole black peppercorns
5 cloves
4 pears, pared

Bring water, lingonberries, sugar and spices to a boil. Lower the heat and simmer the pears until tender, about 15 minutes. Serve warm with vanilla ice cream. 4 servings

Place the fish in a glass dish. Sprinkle with salt, sugar, dill and pepper. Drizzle with Cognac. Cover with plastic wrap and weigh down. Marinate for 2-4 days in the refrigerator. Turn the fish daily.

Mustard sauce: Whisk together mustard, sugar, vinegar and egg yolks. Slowly whisk in the oil until the mixture is emulsified. Season with salt and pepper.

Creamed potatoes: Sauté the onion in butter, then stir in the flour. Whisk in the milk and cream. Simmer for 15 minutes. Add potatoes and dill and heat through. *4 servings*

Previous pages: Ålesund is not just the site of some of Norway's fastest growing small businesses, it is also the center of Norway's fisheries export industry. Ålesund and Kristiansund are known as the klippfish towns. It comes as no surprise that the restaurants in these parts excel when it comes to klippfish dishes.

MAIN COURSE
Klippfish with Basil and Bell Pepper

350 g (12 oz) klippfish (as thick as possible)
1 small bunch fresh basil
1/2 dl (3 1/2 Tbsp) olive oil

Bell pepper oil:
1 yellow bell pepper
1 red bell pepper
2 red onions
3 dl (1 1/4 cups) olive oil
1 Tbsp tomato paste
pinch cayenne pepper
salt and pepper

Potato purée:
almond potatoes
light cream
butter
salt and pepper

Soak the fish in cold water for about four days, changing the water daily. Keep refrigerated.

Cut the fish into four pieces of equal size. Bring a large pot of water to a boil. Add the fish and simmer about 8 minutes. Preheat the oven grill. Purée basil and olive oil in a food processor until smooth. Spread over the fish and grill until bubbly.

Pepper oil: Cut the peppers into strips and chop the onions. Sauté the onion in a small amount of the oil and stir in the tomato paste. Add the pepper strips, cayenne and remaining oil. Simmer 5 minutes. Season with salt and pepper.

Potato purée: Peel the almond potatoes and boil in cream. Mash. Season with butter, salt and pepper.

Divide the potato purée among individual plates. Top with the fish. Spoon the pepper oil all around. Garnish with crispy potato chips, if desired. 4 servings

Thorvald Gulliksen:
GULLIX, ÅLESUND

Over the past 15 years, *Gullix* in Ålesund has built up its reputation as one of the best restaurants between Bergen and Trondheim. *Gullix* is a member of Chaine des Rostisseurs. The restaurant features an international menu, and throughout the year, it arranges special theme weeks.

Thorvald Gulliksen (b. 1943) opened *Gullix* in 1983, after many years of work both in Norway and abroad, including 10 years as chef at *Hotel Alexandra* in Loen from 1973 to 1983.

MAIN COURSE
Bacalao Gullix

500 g (1 1/4 lb) klippfish
2 large onions, sliced
2 garlic cloves, minced
1 1/2 dl (2/3 cup) canned pimientos, drained and chopped
1/2 dried chile pepper, crushed
2 1/2 dl (1 cup) olive oil
flour
1 dl (scant 1/2 cup) tomato paste
1 1/2 dl (2/3 cup) chopped canned tomatoes
5 dl (2 cups) fish stock
salt and pepper

Soak the klippfish in cold water 2-4 days, according to how salty the fish should be, changing water daily. It is a good idea to place the fish on a rack, so the salt that runs off sinks to the bottom. Keep refrigerated.

In a large pot, sauté onion, garlic, pimientos and chili pepper in olive oil. Sprinkle with flour and stir to coat. Stir in tomato paste, chopped tomatoes and fish stock. Simmer 30 minutes, until the sauce is smooth and thick.

Preheat the oven to 200C (400F). Cut the fish into serving pieces and place in a baking dish. Pour the sauce over the fish. Bake about 30 minutes, until the fish is golden and almost flakes.

Serve with boiled potatoes and crusty bread. Have a pepper grinder within reach. *4 servings*

MAIN COURSE
Klippfish Cakes Gullix

400 g (14 oz) cooked klippfish (see previous recipe)
2 1/2 dl (1 cup) mashed potato
2 Tbsp minced onion
salt and pepper

4 carrots, cleaned and sliced
2 Tbsp butter
4 Tbsp (1/4 cup) flour
2 dl (3/4 cup) half and half or full-fat milk

flour
1 egg, lightly beaten
breadcrumbs
olive oil

150 g (5 oz) bacon, cubed and fried until crispy

Chop the fish and combine with potatoes, onions, salt and pepper. Refrigerate 2 hours.

Cook carrots in lightly salted water until tender. Melt the butter and stir in the flour. Whisk in the carrot liquid along with the cream or milk to make a smooth sauce. Strain and stir in the carrots.

Form the fish mixture into patties. Dip in flour, then in egg, then in breadcrumbs. Fry in oil on both sides.

Arrange the fish cakes on individual plates. Sprinkle with bacon. Serve with creamed carrots and boiled potatoes. 4 servings

Bergen is Norway's second-largest city. Many feel that it ranks first in charm, with its old buildings, fjord and archipelago, surrounded by its seven hills. Bergen is an historic city and was Norway's capital during its early period of greatness in the Middle Ages. Fish caught in northern Norway were sold in Bergen for shipment to the European continent, leading Bergen to become one of northern Europe's largest and most important commercial centers during the Hansa period. This colorful port still retains some of that special flavor. The buildings at Bryggen, which are registered on the UNESCO World Heritage List of Cultural Monuments, were first built during that time. The Fish Market, funicular, aquarium and Håkon's Hall are other sights which make Bergen a memorable experience.

Fredrik Hald:
LUCULLUS, BERGEN

Restaurant Lucullus, in the *Hotel Neptune*, has been one of Bergen's most exciting restaurants for many years. The *Neptune's* art collection adds a special ambiance to the rooms and the restaurants. At *Lucullus*, guests can enjoy terrific food surrounded by contemporary and traditional art.

Fredrik Hald (b. 1964) worked at *Restaurant Bellevue* in Bergen, *Bagatelle* in Oslo, and the venerable *Utne Hotel* in Hardanger, before coming to *Lucullus*. Hald gives Norwegian ingredients an international touch, and dessert is his favorite course, because "A bad dessert can ruin a meal."

APPETIZER
Scallops with Oyster Sauce and Asparagus

1 dl (scant 1/2 cup) dry white wine
3 dl (1 1/3 cups) whipping cream
4 oysters, shelled
12 asparagus stalks
butter
salt and pepper
12 scallops, cleaned, roe removed

Combine wine and cream in a saucepan and reduce by half over high heat. Add the raw oysters and any juices. Transfer to a food processor and process until light and frothy. Just before serving, reheat, but do not allow to boil.

Peel the stalk ends of the asparagus. Blanch in lightly salted water for about 3 minutes. Slice diagonally and steam in butter until tender. Sprinkle with salt and pepper.

Grill scallops on both sides. Arrange in a circle on individual plates. Spoon a pile of asparagus in the center. Pour sauce over half the scallops. 4 servings

Right: The strong muscle which holds the scallop's shells together enables it to swim in every direction. Here it hops across the sea floor, trying to escape from a starfish.

DESSERT
Vanilla and Chocolate Bavarian Cream

5 dl (2 cups) full-fat milk
1/2 vanilla bean, split lengthwise
5 egg yolks
1 dl (scant 1/2 cup) sugar
6 sheets (2 Tbsp) gelatin
5 dl (2 cups) whipping cream
100 g (4 oz) semi-sweet chocolate
1 Tbsp strong coffee

Scald the milk with the vanilla bean. Whisk egg yolks and sugar, then whisk in the hot milk. Return to the saucepan and heat carefully, stirring constantly, until thickened. Do not allow to boil.

Soak the gelatin sheets in cold water (sprinkle powdered gelatin over 2 Tbsp of the whipping cream) to soften, about 5 minutes. Squeeze excess water from gelatin sheets (disregard for powdered gelatin) and melt the softened gelatin in the warm vanilla sauce. Strain and allow to cool.

Whip the cream and fold into the cooled vanilla sauce. Pour into individual molds or into a 1 1/2 liter (6 cup) mold. Cover with plastic wrap and freeze. When frozen, unmold and place on a rack.

Melt the chocolate in the coffee. Cool slightly, then pour over the frozen dessert. Arrange individual desserts on plates or slice the large one and serve with fresh berries and berry sauce. 6-8 servings

MAIN COURSE
Redfish with Hazelnut Vinaigrette, Spinach and Parsley Root

2 dl (3/4 cup) hazelnuts
1 egg
1 dl (1/3 cup) balsamic vinegar
4 dl (1 1/3 cups) vegetable oil
salt and pepper

200 g (8 oz) parsley roots
butter
8 spinach clusters or 8 oz fresh spinach leaves
sugar

4 redfish fillets, about 200 g (7-8 oz) each, skin on but scaled
olive oil

Place nuts and egg in the bowl of a food processor. With the motor running, add vinegar and oil in a thin stream until emulsified. Season with salt and pepper. Just before serving, heat carefully, whisking constantly

Clean and julienne the parsley roots. Steam in butter until tender, about 5 minutes. Pluck the spinach leaves from the stalks. Rinse thoroughly in running water. Dry well. Steam until wilted, about 30 seconds. Stir in butter and sugar to taste. Season with salt and pepper.

Sauté the fish, skin side down, in olive oil. Turn and sauté until done or place under the oven grill until sizzling.

Pile the parsley root in the middle of individual plates. Top with the fish. Drizzle dressing all around. Arrange cones of spinach around the edge. 4 servings

Michael Reddington:
STATSRAADEN, SAS RADISSON, BERGEN

Restaurant Statsraaden in the *Radisson SAS Royal Hotel* in Bergen is another hotel restaurant which combines excellent food and local charm. The hotel is part of the old wharf settlement in Bergen, called Bryggen. The oldest buildings on Bryggen date as far back as 1702, and the hotel was designed to fit into the historic setting.

Michael Reddington (b. 1964 in Ireland) came to Norway in 1987 and has been chef at the *Radisson SAS Royal Hotel* in Bergen since 1995. Prior to that time, Reddington worked at hotels and restaurants in Ireland, Switzerland and England.

APPETIZER
Bergen Fish Soup

1 kg (2 1/2 lb) white fish trimmings, preferably from pollack
1 onion, sliced
1 small carrot, chopped
parsley stalks
1 tsp white peppercorns
2 tsp salt
2 liters (quarts) water

60 g (2 oz) butter
1 1/4 dl (1/2 cup) flour
3 dl (1 1/4 cups) whipping cream
3 Tbsp vinegar
1 Tbsp sugar
salt and pepper
1 carrot, julienned
1/2 leek, julienned
300 g (10 oz) tiny fish forcemeat balls
1 dl (scant 1/2 cup) dairy sour cream
parsley

Place fish trimmings, onion, carrot, parsley, peppercorns, salt and water in a pot. Bring to a boil. Skim well. Simmer for 30 minutes. Strain and reduce to 1 liter (quart).

Knead the butter and flour together and whisk into the boiling stock. Whisk until smooth and thickened. Add cream and vinegar and season with sugar, salt and pepper. Return to a boil and simmer over low heat for about 15 minutes. Add carrot and leek and simmer 5 minutes more. Heat the fish forcemeat balls in the soup. Just before serving, stir in the sour cream and sprinkle with parsley. 4 servings

There are many recipes for Bergen fish soup. The one pictured is not the same as the above recipe.

DESSERT
Raspberry Pavlova Roll with Marinated Berries

Marinated Berries:
1 1/4 dl (1/2 cup) sugar
2 1/2 dl (1 cup) water
1/2 cinnamon stick
1/2 vanilla bean
1 star anise
1 strip lemon zest
5 dl (2 cups) mixed fresh berries (blueberries, strawberries,
  up to 1 1/4 dl (1/2 cup) raspberries)

Raspberry Curd:
8 1/2 dl (3 1/2 cups) raspberries
5 eggs
1 1/4 dl (1/2 cup) sugar
115 g (4 oz) unsalted butter

Pavlova:
4 egg whites
3 3/4 dl (1 1/2 cups) confectioner's sugar
30 g (1 oz) semi-sweet chocolate, grated
4 dl (1 2/3 cups) ground hazelnuts
2 Tbsp sugar

Marinated Berries: Bring sugar, water and spices to a boil. Simmer slowly for 15 minutes. Add berries and let steep for at least 1 hour at room temperature.

Raspberry Curd: Purée raspberries in a food mill or press through a sieve. Discard seeds. You will need about 2 1/2 dl (1 cup) purée. Beat eggs and sugar until light and lemon-colored, about 5 minutes. Transfer to a saucepan. Heat, whisking constantly, until thickened. Do not allow to boil. Remove from the heat and beat in the berry purée and the butter. The consistency should be that of smooth buttercream. Chill until needed.

Pavlova: Preheat the oven to 135C (275F). Line a baking sheet with baking parchment. Beat the egg whites with 2 Tbsp confectioner's sugar until soft peaks form. Add remaining sugar and 2/3 of the grated chocolate. Transfer to a pastry bag and pipe into a rectangle on the baking parchment. Combine nuts, sugar and remaining chocolate and sift over. Bake until crispy on top, about 15 minutes. Turn over and peel off parchment. Spread with raspberry butter. Roll up from the long end. Do not refrigerate.

To serve, cut into slices and place in the center of individual plates. Ladle marinated berries all around. 8-10 servings

MAIN COURSE
Citrus-Marinated Cod with Caramelized Onion Mashed Potatoes

700 g (1 1/2 lb) boneless and
* skinless cod fillet*

Marinade:
juice of 1 lime
juice of 1 lemon
juice of 1 orange
2 Tbsp chopped fresh mint
2 Tbsp chopped fresh coriander
1 small garlic clove, minced
1 tsp minced fresh ginger
5 Tbsp (1/3 cup) olive oil
pinch sea salt

Tomato pesto:
1 dl (1/3 cup) olive oil
50 g (1 1/2 oz) dried tomatoes
1 garlic clove, chopped
1 Tbsp pine nuts
2 Tbsp grated Parmesan cheese

Onion mashed potatoes:
400 g (14 oz) potatoes, peeled
1 small onion, sliced
olive oil
2 Tbsp brown sugar
1 Tbsp balsamic vinegar
3-4 Tbsp crème fraîche (or whipping cream)
salt and pepper

Marinated vegetables:
4 thin asparagus tips
1/2 red bell pepper, in strips
1/2 green bell pepper, in strips
1/2 orange bell pepper, in
* strips*
1/2 red onion sliced
1/4 yellow summer squash,
* sliced*
1/4 zucchini, sliced
1/4 eggplant, sliced
1 dl (scant 1/2 cup) olive oil
salt and pepper
1/2 fresh red chile, seeds and
* ribs removed, minced*
chopped fresh coriander
1 dl(scant 1/2 cup) balsamic
* vinegar*

fresh herbs

Cut the fish into four pieces of equal size and place in double plastic bags. Whisk together all the ingredients for the marinade and pour over the fish. Marinate for at least two hours.

Purée all pesto ingredients in a food processor.

Boil the potatoes until tender. Brown the onion in olive oil. Sprinkle with sugar and caramelize. Add vinegar and boil until evaporated. Mash potatoes. Fold in onions and cream and season with salt and pepper.

Brush vegetables with olive oil and sprinkle with salt and pepper. Grill until browned. Transfer to a saucepan and stir in the chile, coriander, vinegar and remaining olive oil. Reheat just before serving.

Sauté the cod. Arrange on individual plates with the vegetables, potatoes and pesto. Garnish with herbs.
4 servings

Kåre Stalheim:
QUALITY BRAKANES HOTEL, ULVIK

Since 1860, *Quality Brakanes Hotel* in Ulvik in Hardanger has been welcoming tourists from Norway and abroad to the Hardanger Fjord, the most famous fjord in western Norway. The magnificent scenery inspired many artists of the national romantic period in the late 19th century, as well as composer Edvard Grieg. During the years just before the turn of the century, many tourist hotels were constructed to accommodate the increasing number of tourists. *Brakanes* was one of the great wooden hotels built at that time. Many were destroyed by fire, including the original *Brakanes*. Today, *Brakanes* and the other hotels along the western fjords offer all the comfort and luxury tourists desire and expect these days, but they still retain their old-fashioned atmosphere. Guests at *Brakanes* can enjoy the spectacular Hardanger scenery from the hotel dining room. Ulvik has been a popular destination for more than 150 years. Apple-blossom time in May is a major photo-opportunity in Hardanger, but the area is also worth a visit at other times of the year.

Kåre Stalheim (b. 1952) has worked in Hordaland county his entire life. He apprenticed at historic *Fleischer's Hotel* in his home town of Voss. After one year at *Hotel Norge* in Bergen, he came to Ulvik, first to *Ulvik Hotel* and then to *Quality Brakanes Hotel*, where he has been chef since 1983.

MAIN COURSE
Salmon á la Brakanes

650 g (1 1/2 lb) boneless and skinless salmon fillet
1/2 red bell pepper
150 g (5 oz) mushrooms
2 carrots
2 Tbsp unsalted butter
1 Tbsp flour
5 dl (2 cups) whipping cream
2 tsp salt
pepper
1 parsley sprig

Cut the salmon into four pieces of equal size. Slice the pepper and mushrooms. Grate the carrot. Melt the butter in a saucepan. Add the vegetables and stir to coat. Add flour, cream, salt and pepper. Simmer 10 minutes. Chop the parsley and add.

Sauté, grill or poach the salmon. Arrange on individual plates with the vegetables and sauce. 4 servings

MAIN COURSE
Hardanger Sea Symphony

1/2 onion
1 green or yellow bell pepper
2 Tbsp vegetable oil
200 g (8 oz) shelled, cooked mussels
200 g (8 oz) shelled, cooked ocean crayfish tails
juice of 1/2 lemon
salt and pepper
650 g (1 1/2 lb) skinless and boneless salmon fillet

Peel the onion and clean pepper. Cut both into julienne. Sauté in oil. Stir in mussels, crayfish tails and lemon juice. Season to taste with salt and pepper.

Cut the salmon into four pieces of equal size. Simmer in salted water until firm, 6-8 minutes.

Serve piping hot with bread. 4 servings

Jan Atle Kalkvik:
LOTHES MAT OG VINHUS, HAUGESUND

Lothes Mat og Vinhus (Lothe's Food and Wine House) is located in an old house dating back to the 1850s. Haugesund is known from Snorre's sagas and was mentioned in connection with the death of Harald Fairhair in the year 930. The burial mound of the King who united Norway is near Karmsund, known as *Kongeveien* (King's Road) in historic times, because kings and chieftains sailed their ships through it to and from the royal estate at Avaldsnes at Karmøy, just south of Hauge-sund.

Jan Atle Kalkvik (b. 1967) grew up in Haugesund and trained in his home county of Rogaland. He also has experience from hotels and other restaurants in the area.

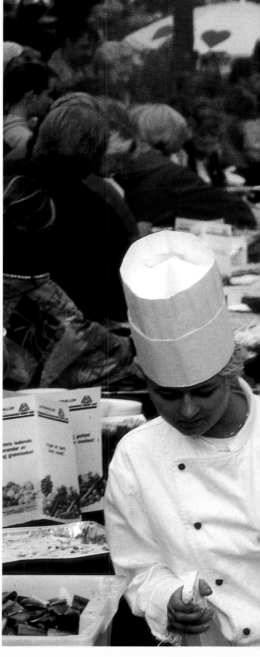

MAIN COURSE
Wild Duck in Beet Sauce with Potato Purée

Beet sauce:
2 medium beets, peeled and
cut into 1 cm (1/2") dice
1 liter (quart) duck stock
1 1/4 dl (1/2 cup) sugar
1 Tbsp raspberry vinegar
2 dl (3/4 cup) whipping
  cream
1 Tbsp cold butter
salt and white pepper

Potato purée:
1 wild duck leg
3 potatoes
1 dl (scant 1/2 cup) whipping
  cream

4 blue potatoes
1 Tbsp clarified butter

700 g (1 2/3 lb) wild duck
  breast

1/2 fennel bulb, diced
1 small wedge red
  cabbage, diced
2 shallots, diced
1 green chile, ribs and
  seeds removed, minced
10 juniper berries,
  crushed

2 Tbsp butter
4 Tbsp (1/4 cup) sugar
1 dl (scant 1/2 cup)
  orange juice

2 black salsify, peeled and
  shredded
2 dl (3/4 cup) olive oil

Beet sauce: Cook the beets in duck stock until tender, about 7 minutes. Caramelize the sugar. Add vinegar and cream and simmer until almost evaporated. Add stock and beets. Reduce by two-thirds over high heat. Beat in the cold butter and season with salt and pepper.

Potato purée: Preheat the oven to 200C (400F). Season the duck leg with salt and pepper and roast about 20 minutes. Remove from the oven and allow to rest for 5 minutes, then roast for 10 minutes more. Peel the potatoes and boil in unsalted water until tender. Remove the meat from the duck leg and grind in a meat grinder with the potatoes. Do not use a food processor. Transfer the mixture to a saucepan, add cream and cook until incorporated.

King of Norway

Peel the blue potatoes and cut into thin slices. Arrange overlapping in eight 7 cm (3") circles on a greased baking sheet. Brush with butter and bake until crispy, 5-7 minutes. Just before serving, reheat at 180C (350F) about 2 minutes. Sandwich together with potato purée.

Season the duck breast and sauté in a grill pan without additional fat, then roast for 10 minutes. Remove from the oven and let rest 5 minutes. Return to the oven and roast 5-10 minutes more. Remove and let rest 5 minutes before serving.

Sauté vegetables, chile and juniper berries in butter. Stir in the sugar and caramelize. Add orange juice and simmer until nearly all liquid has evaporated.

The abundant supply of herring laid the foundation for Haugesund. While herring was once poor man's food in Norway, it has since become a sought-after delicacy. Haugesund may no longer be a herring town, but it does boast of the world's longest herring buffet table.

Deep-fry the salsify shreds in olive oil in several batches. Drain on paper towels. Sprinkle with salt.

To serve, spoon sauce onto individual plates. Arrange vegetables in the center. Arrange diagonal slices of duck breast over the vegetables. Garnish with salsify. Serve the potatoes alongside. 4 servings

APPETIZER
Haugaland Herring Salad with Mushrooms and Rye Rolls

Rye crescent rolls:
2 dl (3/4 cup) beer
4 tsp dry yeast
1 tsp salt
3 Tbsp olive oil
4 dl (1 2/3 cups) all-purpose
  flour
1 3/4 dl (3/4 cup) rye flour
4 dl (1 2/3 cups) whole grain
  rye flour

1 egg
1 Tbsp water

Brine:
1/2 dl (3 Tbsp) water
1 1/2 Tbsp vinegar
1 1/2 Tbsp sugar
1 tsp white pepper

Salad:
1 salt herring fillet
1 dl (scant 1/2 cup) diced
  boiled potato
1 dl (scant 1/2 cup) diced
  roast pork
3 Tbsp diced cooked carrot
3/4 dl (1/3 cup) diced pickled
  beets
1 1/2 Tbsp chopped pickle
1 small apple, peeled, cored
  and diced
1 Tbsp minced leek
1 Tbsp minced onion

80 g (3 oz) button and/or
  oyster mushrooms, julienned
2 hard-cooked eggs, sliced
1 dl (scant 1/2 cup) whipping
  cream
1 Tbsp minced parsley

Rye rolls: Combine beer, yeast, salt and oil in the bowl of an electric mixer with a dough hook. Stir in all the flour. Knead at low speed about 15 minutes. Cover and set in a warm place. Let rise until doubled, about 45 minutes. Punch down and roll out into a circle. Cut into 12 wedge-shaped pieces. Roll each piece, beginning at the wide end. Place on a greased baking sheet, cover and let rise about 45 minutes. Preheat the oven to 200C (400F). Curve the ends to make crescents. Beat egg with water and brush on the rolls. Bake for 10-15 minutes, until golden.

Combine ingredients for brine in a saucepan and heat until the sugar is dissolved. Cool.

Soak the herring fillet in cold water for about 15 minutes. Slice diagonally and place in a bowl. Add remaining salad ingredients. Toss with 2/3 of the brine and refrigerate at least 1 hour.

Combine mushrooms with remaining brine.

Lightly whip the cream and fold in the parsley.

Arrange the salad in the center of individual plates. Garnish with mushrooms, egg slices and parsley cream. Serve with rolls. 4 servings

Alexander W. Utermøhlen:
JANS MAT OG VINHUS, STAVANGER

Jan Ekornes and Harald Osa opened *Jans Mat og Vinhus* (Jan's Food and Wine House) in Stavanger in 1981, and since that time, it has featured the finest food in town. This cellar restaurant at Breitorget incorporates the stone walls of the original foundation from 1820, and at one end are the remains of a well. Even though the number of restaurants in Stavanger has exploded in recent years, *Jans Mat og Vinhus* maintains its position at the top. Each day, it offers a six-course market menu, which accounts for more than 90% of its turnover.

Alexander W. Utermøhlen (b. 1966) traveled to France and the US for international experience after he finished his education and apprenticeship. In 1991, he returned to Stavanger as chef at *Jans Mat og Vinhus*.

MAIN COURSE
Klippfish with Tomato Pesto and Butter Sauce

250 g (8 oz) klippfish
4 plum tomatoes
2 red bell peppers
olive oil
1 onion, chopped
2 garlic cloves, minced
1 Tbsp chopped fresh thyme
salt and pepper
200 g (8 oz) almond or other
  small waxy potatoes

Tomato pesto:
6 sun-dried tomatoes
2 small tomatoes, quartered
2 Tbsp olive oil
1 garlic clove

Butter sauce:
2 dl (3/4 cup) white wine
1 Tbsp chopped shallots
1 tsp white peppercorns
1 small bay leaf
3 1/2 Tbsp whipping cream
100 g (scant 1/2 cup)
  unsalted butter
lemon juice

Soak the klippfish in cold water for three days, changing water daily. Keep refrigerated.

Preheat the oven to 200C (400F). Scald the plum tomatoes in boiling water for about 30 seconds, then peel, seed, and dice. Reserve the seeds. Quarter the peppers, removing the stalks and seeds. Brush with oil. Place on a baking sheet and roast for about 15 minutes. Transfer to a plastic bag for 5 minutes. Peel and dice.

Sauté onion and garlic in oil. Add diced tomatoes, peppers and thyme. Reduce over low heat until thickened. Season with salt and pepper.

Peel and slice the potatoes. Boil until tender.

Tomato Pesto: Chop both kinds of tomatoes. Purée in a food processor with the plum tomato seeds, oil, and garlic. Season to taste.

Butter Sauce: Combine wine, shallots, pepper and bay leaf in a saucepan and reduce until about 3 Tbsp remain. Add cream and bring to a boil. Whisk in the butter in pats. Season with salt, pepper and lemon juice.

Remove the skin and bones from the pre-soaked fish. Steam until almost cooked, about 15 minutes.

Preheat the oven to 160C (320F). Place 7 cm (3") rings (or tuna fish tins with both ends removed) on a greased baking sheet. Layer potatoes, fish and tomato mixture. Repeat until all ingredients are used up. Bake 4 minutes. Transfer to individual plates. Remove the forms. Drizzle with sauce and pesto. Garnish with fresh thyme, if desired. 4 servings

APPETIZER
Pickled Mackerel with Cucumber Yogurt Soup

400 g (14 oz) boneless and skinless mackerel fillet
2 Tbsp salt
2 dl (3/4 cup) water
1 dl (scant 1/2 cup) sugar
2 dl (3/4 cup) white wine vinegar
1 bay leaf
1 tsp coriander seeds
1 tsp pepper
1 star anise
3 shallots, sliced

Cucumber yogurt soup:
2 snake cucumbers
coarse salt
3 dl (1 1/4 cups) full-fat natural yogurt
2 garlic cloves
1 Tbsp lemon juice
3 dl (1 1/4 cups) chicken stock
salt og pepper

2 Tbsp chopped chives
2 Tbsp olive oil

Sprinkle mackerel with salt and let marinate for two hours. Bring water to a boil. Add sugar, vinegar, seasonings and shallots. Remove from the heat. Rinse the fish and slice. Place in the brine. Heat carefully, then remove from the heat. Cool the fish in the brine.

Peel the cucumbers and remove the seeds. Cut into thin slices with a cheese plane. Sprinkle with coarse salt and marinate for one hour. Rinse off the salt and dry by squeezing in a kitchen towel. Place in the bowl of a food processor. Add remaining ingredients and process until smooth. Transfer to a bowl and refrigerate.

Remove the fish from the brine and drain on paper towels. Divide the soup among four individual bowls. Place mackerel slices in the center. Sprinkle with chives and drizzle olive oil over the surface. 4 servings

APPETIZER
Sautéed Scallops with Wild Mushroom Mashed Potatoes and Spinach

8 scallops

2 Tbsp hazelnut oil
1/2 carrot, coarsely chopped
1 shallot, chopped
1/4 leek, chopped
1 Tbsp coriander seeds
1 tsp white peppercorns
1 dl (1/2 cup) white wine
3 dl (1 1/4 cups) fish stock
3 Tbsp unsalted butter
3 Tbsp hazelnut oil

250 g (9 oz) almond potatoes
20 g (2/3 oz) dried porcini mushrooms
1 dl (scant 1/2 cup) whipping cream
3 Tbsp hazelnut oil
salt and pepper

200 g (8 oz) spinach
1 Tbsp butter
1 garlic clove, minced

2 Tbsp hazelnut oil

Open the scallops and remove the white muscle. Rinse and soak in ice water for 20 minutes.

Sauté remaining soft parts of the scallops in hazelnut oil until transparent. Add vegetables and sauté for 2 minutes. Add wine and reduce by three-quarters over high heat. Add fish stock and reduce by half. Strain. Just before serving, whisk in butter and hazelnut oil until light and frothy with an immersion blender. Do not allow to boil.

Peel the potatoes and boil in unsalted water until tender. Drain, stir over heat to dry, then mash. Soak the dried mushrooms in hot water to cover for about 10 minutes. Cook in the cream until tender and stir into the mashed potatoes. Just before serving, reheat and stir in hazelnut oil. Season with salt and pepper.

Rinse the spinach well, removing any coarse stalks. Sauté in butter with garlic. Season to taste.

Sauté scallops in hazelnut oil until golden.

Arrange on individual plates with spinach in the center and scallops all around. Form small potato eggs and place on the plate. Spoon the sauce all around. 4 servings

Stig Juelsen:
N.B. SØRENSEN DAMPSKIBSEXPEDITION, STAVANGER:

N.B.Sørensens Dampskibsexpedition is an exciting eating place. In English, its name translates as the Sørensen Steam Ship Office, the name of the previous business at that address. The first floor is furnished like a busy office, while upstairs is a typical Stavanger living room from around the turn of the century. The restaurant's unique atmosphere is enhanced by all the interesting artifacts from the old shipping office.

Stig Juelsen (b. 1965) worked at both *Spisestedet Feinschmecker* and *Royal Christiania* in Oslo before he came to Stavanger in 1993. In keeping with old steamship tradition, Juelsen often travels abroad for inspiration and new ideas.

MAIN COURSE
Marinated Cod on a Warm Tomato-Feta Salad

Harissa:
1/2 red chile or 1 small dried chile
juice of 1/2 lime
1/2 Tbsp cumin
1/2 Tbsp ground coriander
4 garlic cloves
1 dl (1/3 cup) mint leaves with stalks, packed
1/2 tsp sea salt
1 1/2 Tbsp white wine vinegar
about 1 dl (1/3 cup) olive oil

800 g (1 3/4 lb) boneless cod fillet, skin on
salt
extra virgin olive oil

Tomato-feta salad:
1 red onion, coarsely chopped
2 dl (3/4 cup) extra virgin olive oil
6 plum tomatoes, each cut into 6 wedges
250 g (8 oz) feta cheese, cubed
10 kalamata olives
juice of 2 limes
30-40 leaves flat-leaf parsley

Watercress or dill, parsley, arugula, fresh coriander

Harissa: Combine all ingredients in a mortar or a blender. Do not use a food processor. Steep at room temperature for at least 12 hours.

Preheat the oven to 200C (400F). Remove the skin from the cod. Scrape so that no flesh remains. Place on a greased baking sheet. Sprinkle with salt. Place another greased baking sheet on top of the fish skin, weighing it down. Bake for 5 minutes. Remove the top baking sheet, brush fish skin with olive oil and bake until brown and crispy, 7-10 minutes.

Divide the cod fillet into four pieces of equal size. Spread with a thin layer of harissa. Sprinkle with salt. Marinate for 30 minutes. Sauté in oil. Do not allow the harissa to burn. Let the fish rest for a couple of minutes before serving.

Tomato-feta salad: Sauté the onion in oil until transparent in a different pan. Fold in remaining ingredients except parsley.

To serve, spoon the salad on individual plates and drizzle with pan juices. Top with fish. Garnish with "sails" of fish skin and watercress or other herbs.
4 servings

APPETIZER

Sardines and Ocean Crayfish on Tapenade Toast

Batter:
3 egg yolks
1 dl (scant 1/2 cup) beer
3 1/4 dl (1 1/3 cups) cornstarch
5 dl (2 cups) flour
1 Tbsp blackening spices
salt and pepper

Blackening spices for fish
(enough for many servings):
1 Tbsp crushed, crispy-fried
  onions
1 garlic clove, minced
1 Tbsp ground paprika
1 Tbsp dried thyme
1/2 Tbsp dried oregano
1/2 Tbsp cayenne pepper
1/2 Tbsp salt
1 tsp ground black pepper

8 large ocean crayfish

Tapenade:
400 g (14 oz) black olives,
  preferably kalamatas
3 garlic cloves
1 Tbsp capers
8 anchovy fillets
2 dl (3/4 cup) extra virgin olive oil

Crayfish stock:
shells from 8 ocean crayfish
vegetable oil
3 Tbsp Cognac
1 liter (quart) veal stock
1 carrot, chopped
1 celery stalk, chopped
2 onions, chopped
2 leeks, chopped
1/3 tsp cayenne pepper
2 tsp ground paprika
2 Tbsp fresh rosemary
1 Tbsp fresh thyme
1 whole garlic bulb, separated
  into cloves but not peeled
1 bay leaf
3 Tbsp tomato paste

4 slices white bread
olive oil
parsley

8 whole sardines, gutted
Vegetable oil

Whisk egg yolks and beer. Add cornstarch, flour and spices, mixing lightly. Let rest at least 2 hours.

Place the first four tapenade ingredients in a food processor. With the motor running, add the oil in a thin stream until emulsified. Store in the refrigerator.

Clean the crayfish and refrigerate the tails for later use. Crush the shells and sauté in oil in a saucepan. Pour over Cognac and ignite. Add veal stock and bring to a boil. Add remaining ingredients. Return to a boil and simmer for 20 minutes. Strain and reduce by two-thirds over high heat.

Sauté the bread in olive oil. Cool. Spread with a thick layer of tapenade and place on individual plates.

Dip the crayfish tails and the sardines in the batter, then fry in oil until golden. Drain on paper towels. Deep-fry the parsley.

Top the toast with sardines, crayfish tails and parsley. Spoon the crayfish reduction all around. 4 servings

DESSERT

Pears Poached in Port Wine in Crisp Pastry with Chocolate Ice Cream

Port wine syrup:
5 dl (2 cups) Port wine
3 3/4 dl (1 1/2 cups) sugar
1 tsp minced fresh ginger
1 vanilla bean
1 cinnamon stick
juice of 2 limes

1 1/2 dl (2/3 cup) raisins

Chocolate ice cream:
5 dl (2 cups) whipping cream
5 dl (2 cups) full-fat milk
1 3/4 dl (3/4 cup) sugar
9 egg yolks
200 g (7 oz) semi-sweet chocolate

Mint oil:
1 dl (1/3 cup) fresh mint
  leaves, packed
1 dl (1/3 cup) safflower or corn
  oil

8 pears

4 egg roll wrappers or 4 sheets
  filo pastry
vegetable oil
sugar

Combine all ingredients for the Port wine syrup and bring to a boil. Add raisins and let steep for about two hours.

Chocolate ice cream: Scald cream, milk and sugar. Whisk the egg yolks lightly. Slowly whisk in the milk until well-combined. Chop the chocolate and add, stirring occasionally until melted. Chill. Freeze in an ice cream machine.

Mint oil: Steep the mint leaves for about 15 seconds in boiling water. Transfer immediately to ice water. Squeeze out as much water as possible and place in a blender. Do not use a food processor. With the motor running, slowly add the oil. Let run for 3-4 minutes. Steep for at least 3 hours.

Peel and core the pears. Slice into thin wedges. Bring the Port wine syrup to a boil and add the pears. Simmer for about 15 minutes. Cool. Drain the pears, returning the syrup to a saucepan. Reduce by half over high heat. Use as a sauce.

Preheat the oven to 150C (300F). Defrost the pastry. Dip the pastry sheets into vegetable oil, then sprinkle with sugar. Form into a basket inside 8 greased coffee cups. Bake until golden, about 5 minutes.

Place half the pears in the baskets with ice cream, then another layer of pears and raisins. Drizzle sauce all around. Garnish with mint oil and shredded mint leaves. 8 servings

Hans Morten Mathiassen:
RESTAURANT CARTELLET, STAVANGER:

Cartellet is in the cellar of the *Rica Hotel Victoria* in Stavanger, a building which was completed at the end of the last century. The restaurant interior combines rustic large stones, brick and antique tiles with elegant furnishings in surprising harmony. *Cartellet* bases its menu on the culinary traditions of Rogaland, accented by the Mediterranean and Asian kitchens.

Hans Morten Mathiassen (b. 1964) has had a many-faceted career over the past 20 years, including a stint as chef at the *Radisson SAS* hotels in Stavanger. He is active in the Chefs' Guild and has been given the title of honor, "Cordon Bleu."

MAIN COURSE
Sautéed Plaice with Garlic and Baked Tomatoes

1 plaice or other flat fish, about 2 kg (2 1/4 lb)
8 garlic cloves
2 Tbsp olive oil
3 Tbsp unsalted butter
24 cherry tomatoes
1 Tbsp finely chopped parsley
1 Tbsp finely chopped fresh rosemary leaves
salt and pepper

Clean the fish, removing the head and fins. Scrape the darker side with a sharp knife. Rinse well. Divide lengthwise, following the stripe on the back. Remove the skin on the lighter side. Cut each half into four pieces.

Peel the garlic and place in a saucepan with cold water to cover. Bring to a boil. Drain. Repeat twice.

Preheat the oven to 200C (400F). Heat a skillet which can be used in the oven. Add oil and butter. Sauté the fish, dark side down. Add remaining ingredients. Cover and bake in the oven for 10-15 minutes.

Remove fish, tomatoes and garlic from the pan and arrange (skin side up) on individual plates. Stir fresh herbs into the pan juices and pour over the fish. Serve with boiled potatoes. 4 servings

MAIN COURSE
Coriander-Sautéed Pollack with Grilled Scallops, Creamed Corn and Red Wine Juices

2 shallots, minced
2 dl (3/4 cup) red wine
1 dl (1/3 cup) beef stock
2 Tbsp cold unsalted butter
salt and pepper
1 cob fresh corn
1 dl (1/3 cup) whipping cream
1 tsp chopped fresh thyme
400 g (14 oz) boneless and skinless pollack fillets
1/2 tsp coriander seeds, crushed
olive oil
4 scallops, cleaned and roe removed

Combine shallots and wine and reduce over high heat until about 3 Tbsp remain. Add stock and reduce a few minutes more. Beat in the butter and season with salt and pepper. Do not allow the sauce to boil after butter is added.

Cut the corn from the cob and combine with cream in a saucepan. Cook until tender and most of the liquid has evaporated, about 5 minutes. Stir in the thyme and season with salt and pepper.

Cut the fish into four pieces of equal size. Season with coriander, salt and pepper. Sauté in oil until golden on both sides. Grill scallops on both sides in a grill pan.

Divide the creamed corn among four individual plates. Place fish in the center, then top with the scallops. Spoon red wine sauce all around. 4 servings

DESSERT
Rosemary-Baked Apples with Calvados Sorbet

1 sheet (3 oz) puff pastry
2 Tbsp confectioner's sugar
4 tart apples, peeled, cored and cut into wedges
1 tsp grated orange zest
2 Tbsp unsalted butter
4 Tbsp (1/4 cup) sugar
1 Tbsp finely chopped fresh rosemary leaves

Rosemary custard sauce:
2 1/2 dl (1 cup) full-fat milk
2 1/2 dl (1 cup) whipping cream
5 egg yolks
1 1/2 dl (2/3 cup) sugar
1 dl (1/3 cup) cut fresh rosemary leaves

Calvados sorbet:
200 g (7 oz) apple cuttings (peel, cores) or 1 large apple
1 dl (scant 1/2 cup) sugar
3 dl (1 1/4 cups) water
1/2 Tbsp glucose
2 Tbsp Calvados

4 rosemary sprigs

Preheat the oven to 220C (425F). Line a baking sheet with baking parchment. Roll out the puff pastry on a lightly floured board and sprinkle with confectioner's sugar. Divide into four equal parts. Place on prepared sheet and bake until golden and puffed, about 4 minutes. Cool on a rack.

Cook apple wedges in a saucepan with the orange rind, butter, sugar and rosemary until tender, about 8 minutes.

Rosemary custard sauce: Scald milk and cream. Whisk eggs and sugar lightly together. Slowly add the hot milk mixture. Return to the saucepan and bring almost to a boil, stirring constantly. Strain immediately. Let cool. Stir in the rosemary leaves.

Calvados sorbet: Cook the apple cuttings, sugar and water 10-15 minutes. Strain, reserving liquid. Add glucose and Calvados. Chill, then freeze in an ice cream maker.

To serve, place a crispy puff pastry base on each plate. Top with apples, then sorbet. Spoon sauce all around. Garnish with a rosemary sprig. 4 servings

Roy Parker:
LUIHN, KRISTIANSAND

Restaurant Luihn is doing its share to put Kristiansand on the Norwegian restaurant map. It is located by the square which was the site of the town gallows until 1819. Nearby, a small heart on the pavement marks the center of town, and *Luihn* uses this heart in its logo. The restaurant's friendly ambiance and varied menu, which features both fish and meat dishes, changes monthly.

Roy Parker (b. 1952 in England) came to Norway in 1976 to work as a cook at the *Caledonien Hotel* in Kristiansand. Since then, he has stayed in the capital of Sørlandet. Since 1992, he has been both manager and chef at *Restaurant Luihn*.

APPETIZER
Baked Turbot with Vegetable Nage

300 g (10 oz) skinless and boneless fillet of turbot
fresh thyme
salt and pepper
3 dl (1 1/4 cup) fresh breadcrumbs
100 g (3 oz) unsalted butter
5 dl (2 cups) fish stock
3 dl (1 1/4 cups) apple juice or cider
juice of 1 lemon
1 leek
6 green asparagus stalks
1 zucchini
2 black salsify
1 small celeriac

Preheat the oven to 200C (400F). Place the turbot skin-side down in a greased baking dish. Sprinkle with thyme, salt, pepper and crumbs. Dot with 2 Tbsp of the butter. Bake for 10 minutes.

Combine stock, apple juice and lemon juice. Reduce by half over high heat. Cut the vegetables into large chunks and add. Cook until tender. Remove and keep warm. Beat the remaining butter into the stock and season to taste.

Ladle the enriched stock into deep plates. Top with fish. Serve immediately. 4 servings

Left: Welcome to Sørlandet and Farsund.

MAIN COURSE
Shepherd's Pie

500 g (1 1/4 lb) ground lamb
1 small onion, minced
1/2 tsp dried thyme
1/2 tsp dried basil
1/2 tsp dried rosemary
1 tsp tomato paste
3 dl (1 1/4 cups) lamb stock
1 tsp cornstarch stirred into 1 tsp cold stock or water

Potato purée:
1 kg (2 1/4 lb) potatoes
100 g (3 oz) butter
1 egg
salt and pepper

Brown the lamb with the onion and herbs without additional fat. Stir in the tomato paste. Add the stock and simmer slowly for one hour. Strain. Stir the cornstarch mixture into the stock and cook until thickened. Stir in the meat and onions. Pour into a greased baking dish.

Preheat the oven to 200C (400F). Peel the potatoes and boil in unsalted water until tender. Mash with butter, egg, salt and pepper. Spoon into a pastry tube and pipe all over the meat mixture. Brush with butter. Bake for about 10 minutes, until golden. Serve with fresh vegetables. 4 servings

MAIN COURSE
Salmon Steamed in Red Wine with Mushrooms and Spinach

800 g (1 3/4 lb) boneless and skinless salmon fillet
2 dl (3/4 cup) red wine
4 dl (1 2/3 cups) whipping cream
100 g (3 oz) unsalted butter
150 g (5 oz) mushrooms, cleaned and sliced
150 g (5 oz) tiny spinach leaves
salt and pepper

Remove any small bones from the salmon. Divide into four pieces of equal size. Bring the red wine to a boil. Add the salmon and cover. Lower heat and simmer for 5 minutes. Remove the salmon from the pan and keep warm. Add the cream and reduce over high heat for 5-6 minutes. Gradually beat in all but 2 Tbsp of the butter. Do not allow the sauce to boil.

Brown the mushrooms in the remaining butter. Toward the end of the cooking time, add the spinach. Season with salt and pepper.

To serve, divide the mushrooms and spinach among individual plates. Top with fish and spoon sauce all around. Serve with boiled almond potatoes. 4 servings

Jarl Vøllestad:
RESTAURANT BAKGÅRDEN, KRISTIANSAND

Restaurant Bakgården in Kristiansand calls itself "the place for those who enjoy life." The ambiance, with a fireplace in the open kitchen and the flickering light of candles in the old-fashioned decor, makes guests feel right at home. The menu, with courses ranging from the traditional to the exotic, is written with chalk on the wall.

Jarl Vøllestad (b. 1959) studied in Kristiansand. Since then, he has been delighting the people of southern Norway with his artistry in the kitchen. He has been chef and manager of *Restaurant Bakgården* since 1988.

MAIN COURSE
Peppered Monkfish

800 g (1 3/4 lb) trimmed monkfish
canned green pepper berries, drained
freshly ground coarse salt and white pepper
3 eggs
butter
4 tomatoes
1 Tbsp chopped fresh basil
3 dl (1 1/4 cups) whipping cream

Cut the fish into four pieces of equal size. Press a generous amount of pepper berries into the fish. Sprinkle with salt and pepper. Whisk the eggs lightly, then dip the fish, coating well. Fry in butter on both sides.

Scald the tomatoes in boiling water for about 30 seconds, then peel, seed and dice.
Remove the fish from the pan and keep warm. Add the tomatoes, basil and cream. Simmer until thickened, about 5 minutes. Season to taste.

Serve with potatoes or rice and buttered vegetables.
4 servings

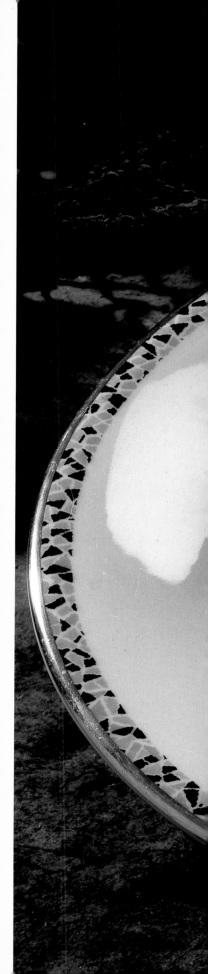

MAIN COURSE
Baked Salmon

800 g (1 3/4 lb) salmon fillet, from the thickest part, skin on.
100 g (4 oz) Parma ham, in thin slices
100 g (4 oz) Parmesan cheese, in thin slices or slivers
1 Tbsp dry mustard
3 Tbsp olive oil
1 tsp chopped thyme
salt and pepper
dry breadcrumbs

Sauce:
juice of 2 limes
1 tsp minced fresh ginger
4 Tbsp (1/4 cup) honey
400 g (14 oz) unsalted butter

Preheat the oven to 220C (425F). Remove any tiny bones from the fish. Slice the fish halfway through at 2 cm (3/4") intervals and fill pockets with ham and cheese. Whisk the mustard into the oil and brush over the fish. Sprinkle with thyme, salt, pepper and breadcrumbs. Bake for about 15 minutes. Allow the fish to rest for about 5 minutes before serving.

Sauce: Combine lime juice, ginger and honey in a saucepan and reduce by half over high heat. Lower heat and beat in the butter in pats. Do not allow the sauce to boil.

Serve the fish with sauce, potatoes and a green salad.
4 servings

DESSERT
Raspberry Bavarian Cream with Tropical Fruit Salsa

4 dl (1 3/4 cups) fresh raspberries
1 dl (scant 1/2 cup) water
4 Tbsp (1/4 cup) sugar
3 egg yolks
3 sheets (tsp powdered) gelatin
2 1/2 dl (1 cup) whipping cream

5 dl (2 cups) diced mixed tropical fruit, such as papaya, mango, kiwi, pineapple, melon, passion fruit

Marinade:
3 Tbsp tequila
3 Tbsp lime juice

1 1/2 dl (1/2 cup) fresh raspberries
fresh mint leaves

Combine berries, water and sugar and bring to a boil. Simmer for one minute, until the sugar has dissolved. Press the mixture through a sieve, discarding the small pits. Whisk the egg yolks and stir in the berry purée. Soak the gelatin sheets in cold water (or sprinkle powdered gelatin over 1 Tbsp cold water) to soften, about 5 minutes. Squeeze excess water from the gelatin sheets (disregard for powdered gelatin) and melt. Stir into the berry mixture. Whip the cream and fold in lightly but thoroughly. Pour into individual molds and refrigerate until set, at least 3 hours. Unmold onto dessert dishes.

Combine diced tropical fruit with tequila and lime juice. Marinate for at least 3 hours.

Serve the fruit with the Bavarian cream. Garnish with fresh berries and mint leaves. 4 servings

Odd Ivar Solvold:
LUDL'S GOURMET ODD IVAR SOLVOLD, SANDEFJORD

When *Ludl's Gourmet* opened in Sandefjord, it was the first Norwegian gourmet restaurant outside Oslo and Bergen. Edgar Ludl, originally from Austria, had become a prominent figure in Norwegian gastronomy while at *Park Hotell* in Sandefjord. There were great expectations when he decided to go out on his own. Twenty years ago, it was not easy to run a restaurant of Ludl's caliber in a small Norwegian town. But it did not take long before the reputation of *Ludl's Gourmet* had spread far beyond the area of Vestfold.

Odd Ivar Solvold (b. 1969) is another chef who apprenticed at *Park Hotell*. After he won a silver medal at the World Championships for young cooks, Edgar Ludl hired him to work at *Ludl's Gourmet*. Today, Solvold owns the restaurant. Odd Ivar Solvold has many medals from international competitions. He has won three Norwegian cooking championships and has won both gold and silver with the Norwegian culinary team at the American Culinary Classic and the Culinary Olympics. Odd Ivar Solvold is team leader for the Norwegian Culinary Team through the year 2000. In 1995, he was named Chef of the Year in Norway. He is carrying on the tradition of *Ludl's Gourmet* as one of Norway's finest restaurants.

Lukewarm Jarlsberg Tart.
Recipe on following page.

99

APPETIZER
Lukewarm Jarlsberg Tart

Tart shell:
5 dl (2 cups) flour
150 g (5 oz) butter
1 egg
3 Tbsp water
salt

Filling:
5 Tbsp (1/3 cup) minced
  shallot
2 Tbsp butter
3 eggs
2 dl (3/4 cup) whipping cream
6 dl (2 1/2 cups) grated
  Jarlsberg cheese
cayenne pepper
freshly ground white pepper
2 Tbsp chopped chives

Celery oil:
2 celery stalks, peeled and cut
  into 2 cm (3/4") lengths
5 dl (2 cups) water
2 tsp salt
1 dl (1/3 cup) walnut oil
freshly ground white pepper

Red bell pepper pesto:
1 red bell pepper, cored
1 Tbsp oil
1 garlic clove, peeled and
  blanched for 5 minutes
3 Tbsp pine nuts
1 dl (1/3 cup) olive oil

Mild goat cheese cream:
100 g (4 oz) soft fresh goat
  cheese
1 Tbsp cottage cheese
1 Tbsp chopped chives

Tart shell: Place all ingredients in a food processor. Pulse until the mixture just holds together. Gather into a ball, wrap in plastic and refrigerate for at least 1 hour. Roll out to 2-3 mm (1/16") on a floured board. Press into a 24 cm (10") tart pan with 3 cm (1 1/4") high sides. Trim.

Filling: Preheat the oven to 180C (350F). Sauté the shallot in butter. Whisk eggs and cream, then add remaining ingredients. Pour into the tart shell. Bake about 25 minutes, until set.

Celery oil: Bring water and salt to a boil. Add celery and cook for 3 minutes. Remove and plunge immediately into ice water. Drain, then place in a food processor. With the motor running, slowly add the walnut oil to make a thick sauce. Season with pepper.

Bell pepper pesto: Preheat the oven to 200C (400F). Rub the pepper with oil and salt. Bake for about 10 minutes, until the peel blisters. Plunge into ice water. Peel, remove seeds and ribs and cut into chunks. Place in a food processor with the garlic and pine nuts. With the motor running, slowly add the oil until thick and creamy. Season with salt and pepper.

Goat cheese cream: Purée goat cheese and cottage cheese in a food processor until smooth. Stir in the chives and season with salt and pepper.

To serve, cut the tart into wedges and place on individual plates. Top with cheese cream and garnish with celery oil and bell pepper pesto. 4 servings

APPETIZER
Cod and Ocean Crayfish Pizza

Crusts:
1 dl (scant 1/2 cup) olive oil
salt
1 dl (scant 1/2 cup) water
20 g (3/4 oz) fresh yeast
4 dl (1 2/3 cups) all-purpose
  flour

Olive purée:
1 3/4 dl (3/4 cup) pitted black
  olives
4 anchovy fillets
1 Tbsp capers
1 garlic clove, blanched
  5 minutes
3 Tbsp olive oil

Spinach and parmesan cream:
1 garlic clove, sliced
1 dl (scant 1/2 cup) extra virgin olive oil
100 g (4 oz) fresh spinach leaves, rinsed and dried, coarse
  stalks removed
3 Tbsp grated Parmesan cheese

Filling:
400 g (14 oz) boneless and
  skinless cod fillets
salt
water
freshly ground white pepper
3 Tbsp olive oil

8 ocean crayfish
1/4 tsp sweet paprika
salt and freshly ground pepper
3 Tbsp olive oil
chervil

Crusts: Combine oil, salt, water and yeast. Gradually add flour. Knead until smooth and elastic. Cover and let rest in a warm place for about 30 minutes. Preheat the oven to 200C (400F). Line a baking sheet with baking parchment. Divide the dough in half. Reserve one half for another use. Divide the other half into four equal pieces. Roll each into 10 cm (4") circles. Pinch to form an edge. Place on the prepared sheet. Bake for 10 minutes.

Olive purée: Place olives, anchovies, capers and the cooked garlic clove in a food processor. With the motor running, slowly add the olive oil to make a thick cream.

Spinach and parmesan cream: Sauté garlic in olive oil. Add the spinach and salt. Sauté until wilted. Place in a food processor with the parmesan and process to a smooth cream.

Filling: Poach half the cod in lightly salted water 7-8 minutes. Drain. Season the remaining fish with salt and pepper and sauté in hot olive oil until crispy, about 5 minutes. Season the crayfish with paprika, salt and pepper, and sauté in oil.

To serve, spread a layer of spinach-parmesan cream on each pizza crust. Top with poached cod, then crayfish and then fried fish. Garnish with a spoonful of olive purée and chervil. 4 servings

DESSERT
Semi-Frozen Apple-Spice Cream with Candied Apricots

Apple cream:
4 tart apples, peeled, cored and diced
1 dl (scant 1/2 cup) water
1 cinnamon stick
1 1/4 dl (1/2 cup) sugar
1/2 dl (3 Tbsp) Calvados
2 1/2 dl (1 cup) whipping cream

Raspberry-vanilla sauce:
2 1/2 dl (1 cup) water
5 dl (2 cups) raspberries
1 1/2 dl (2/3 cup) sugar
1/2 vanilla bean

Basil-cinnamon sorbet:
1/2 dl (3 Tbsp) water
2 1/2 dl (1 cup) sugar
1 cinnamon stick
1 bunch fresh basil
2 Tbsp glucose
juice of 1/2 lemon

Crispy layers:
3/4 dl (1/3 cup) all-purpose flour
1 egg

Candied apricots:
12 fresh apricots
5 dl (2 cups) water
2 1/2 dl (1 cup) sugar
pinch saffron
1/2 vanilla bean, split lengthwise

Caramel cups:
125 g (4 oz) butter (room temperature)
1 1/2 dl (2/3 cup) sugar
1 1/4 dl (1/2 cup) all-purpose flour
3-4 Tbsp half and half or light cream

Sour cream topping:
1/2 dl (3 Tbsp) dairy sour cream (do not use low-fat
 sour cream)
1 1/2 Tbsp confectioner's sugar

Garnish:
1 3/4 dl (3/4 cup) raspberries
mint leaves or lemon balm

Apple cream: Place apples in a saucepan with water, cinnamon and sugar and bring to a boil. Simmer until soft. Press through a sieve. Cool. Stir in the Calvados. Whip the cream and fold into the apple mixture. Divide among four individual serving rings/forms, about 7 cm (3") in diameter. Freeze.

Raspberry-vanilla sauce: Bring water and berries to a boil. Mash berries and press through a sieve. Add sugar to the juice and bring to a simmer. Skim frequently, until the sauce is transparent. Split the vanilla bean, scrape out the seeds and add. Reduce over high heat until syrupy.

Basil-cinnamon sorbet: Bring water, sugar and cinnamon to a boil. Remove from the heat and let steep about 2 hours. Strain. When completely cool, pour into a food processor. Add basil, glucose and lemon juice. Purée until smooth. Freeze in an ice cream maker.

Crispy layers: Preheat the oven to 170C (330F). Combine ingredients with a hand mixer. Make small tartlets in miniature muffin tins. Bake until golden, about 5 minutes.

Candied apricots: Halve the apricots and remove the pits. Bring water, sugar, saffron and vanilla to a boil. Add apricots and simmer until the skin splits. Remove from the syrup and peel. Allow to cool.

Caramel cups: Preheat the oven to 180C (350F). Line a baking sheet with baking parchment. Combine all ingredients and beat until smooth. Spoon circles onto prepared sheet. Bake until golden, about 5 minutes. As soon as the cookies are removed from the oven, drape over teacups to form bowls. Cool.

Sour cream topping: Whip sour cream with confectioner's sugar until stiff.

To serve, arrange apple cream, apricots and sorbet with crispy layers in between. Fill caramel cups with sour cream topping and raspberries. Drizzle raspberry sauce and apricot syrup all around. Garnish with mint or lemon balm.

Arne Sagedal:
BREISETH HOTEL, LILLEHAMMER

The 1994 Winter Olympics made Lillehammer a household word around the world, but the districts around the Olympic town have held special appeal for artists for many years. The valleys north of Lake Mjøsa have provided solitude and inspiration for generations of painters and writers. *Breiseth Hotell*, in the center of town, still has an old-fashioned turn-of-the-century feel. The well-known Lillehammer school of painters used to meet at *Breiseth*, and many original pictures from that time keep their spirits alive. Many other paintings from the same period are on view across the street at the Lillehammer Art Museum. The restaurant at *Breiseth*, *Thorvalds Bar & Spiseri* (Thorvald's bar and eatery) is named after the painter Thorvald Erichsen.

Arne Sagedal (b. 1957) trained at the *Grand Hotel* in Oslo, where he worked until 1988. Then he moved to Lillehammer, where he was chef at *Oppland Hotel* for four years and then he spent two years as manager of *Mormors Hus* (Grandmother's House). After two years at *Holmenkollen Park Hotel Rica* in Oslo, he returned to Lillehammer to take over as chef at *Breiseth Hotell* in 1996.

APPETIZER
Chile Shrimp in Filo Pastry with Eggplant and Gazpacho Sauce

300 g (10 oz) cooked shelled tiny shrimp
juice of 1 lime
1 tsp grated fresh ginger
1 fresh red chile, seeds and ribs removed, finely chopped
4 sheets filo pastry or 4 spring roll wrappers
olive oil
pepper

Gazpacho sauce:
1 red bell pepper
1 celery stalk
1 small zucchini
2 shallots
2 garlic cloves
2 dl (3/4 cup) tomato juice
salt and pepper

Fried eggplant:
1 small eggplant
olive oil
salt and pepper

fresh coriander

Preheat the oven to 200C (400F). Combine shrimp, lime juice, ginger and chili. Cut the filo pastry into quarters to make 16 squares. Brush with oil and place a spoonful of the shrimp mixture on each. Twist the ends. Brush with oil and sprinkle with pepper. Bake for 5 minutes, until golden.

Gazpacho sauce: Clean and dice the pepper, celery and zucchini. Mince the shallots and garlic. Sauté in oil until soft but not brown. Add tomato juice. Bring to a boil. Season with salt and pepper.

Fried eggplant: Slice the eggplant. Sauté in oil. Season with salt and pepper.

To assemble, place eggplant slices diagonally across individual plates. Top each with four shrimp "bonbons." Spoon sauce all around. Garnish with coriander. 4 servings

APPETIZER
Grilled Marinated Salmon with Root Vegetable Purée and a Dill/Horseradish Reduction

Marinated salmon:
2 tsp sugar
3 tsp salt
freshly ground white pepper
2 tsp finely crushed juniper berries
400 g (14 oz) skinless and boneless salmon fillet
vegetable oil

Dill/horseradish reduction:
1 shallot, minced
unsalted butter
2 dl (3/4 cup) white wine
2 dl (3/4 cup) fish stock
2-3 Tbsp grated horseradish
1 dl (scant 1/2 cup) chopped dill
1 Tbsp butter

Root vegetable purée:
150 g (5 oz) almond potatoes
1/2 carrot
3 Tbsp butter
1 Tbsp whipping cream
salt and pepper

Marinated salmon: Combine sugar, salt, pepper and juniper berries in a plastic bag. Add the fish and marinate overnight in the refrigerator.

Dill/horseradish reduction: Sauté the shallot until golden. Add wine and stock. Reduce over high heat until half the original amount remains. Stir in the horseradish. Cool. Place the dill in a food processor. Add the horseradish stock and process until smooth. Heat. Whisk in the butter just before serving. Do not allow the sauce to boil.

Root vegetable purée: Peel and cook the potatoes and carrot until tender. Mash with butter and cream. Season with salt and pepper. Keep warm.

Just before serving, cut the marinated salmon into four triangles. Brush with oil and grill on both sides in a grill pan. Divide the root vegetable purée among four individual plates. Top with the fish. Drizzle horseradish-dill reduction all around. 4 servings

MAIN COURSE
Roedeer Filet with Chanterelle Fricassee and Port Wine Sauce

600 g (1 1/3 lb) trimmed roedeer filet – 2 filets
salt and pepper
butter
1 carrot
1 parsley root
1/4 small rutabaga
1 pork caul 40x20 cm (16x8")
1 Tbsp fresh thyme
1 Tbsp fresh rosemary

Deep-fried salsify:
1 black salsify
vegetable oil

Port wine sauce:
2 Tbsp sugar
3 Tbsp balsamic vinegar
2 dl (3/4 cup) Port wine
1 dl (scant 1/2 cup) red wine
2 dl (3/4 cup) rich beef or game stock
2 Tbsp butter

Chanterelle fricassee:
200 g (8 oz) small chanterelles
24 tiny onions
vegetable oil
2 tomatoes
1 tsp chopped chives

Season the meat with salt and pepper. Brown in butter. Clean and julienne the root vegetables. Blanch in lightly salted water with a pat of butter for about one minute. Spread out the caul and arrange the vegetables on it. Top with the meat. Fold the caul over the meat and vegetables. Brown in butter over low heat.

Deep-fried salsify: Cut the salsify into thin ribbons lengthwise with a potato peeler. Fry the ribbons in oil until crispy and golden. Drain on paper towels.

Port wine sauce: Caramelize the sugar in a saucepan. Stir in the vinegar. Add Port and red wine. Reduce until syrupy. Add the stock. Whisk in the butter and season to taste. Keep warm but do not allow to boil.

Preheat the oven to 200C (400F). Roast the roedeer for 6-8 minutes. Remove from the oven and let rest 5 minutes. Then roast 2 minutes more.

Clean chanterelles and onions and sauté in oil. Pour off the oil. Scald the tomatoes in boiling water for about 30 seconds, then peel, seed and dice. Add to the mushroom mixture with the chives.

Slice the roedeer roll so that each portion consists of three medallions of different heights. Arrange on individual plates with deep fried salsify in the center. Spoon sauce and chanterelle fricassee around the meat. Serve with hash brown potatoes. 4 servings

At an elevation of 650 meters above sea level, Røros is Norway's highest mountain town. There are many reasons to visit Røros. The old mining town is one of four Norwegian sites registered on the UNESCO World Heritage List of Cultural Monuments, which includes other wonders such as the pyramids at Giza and the palace at Versailles.

The discovery of iron ore and the opening of the mine during the 1600s formed the economic basis for this town on the inhospitable Røros plateau. The mine has been closed for years, but the town, rendered immortal in the paintings of Harald Sohlberg and the literary works of Johan Falkberget, still stands. Nature and culture come together in Røros, which has become a gathering place for artisans of all kinds. Behind the log walls of the many old wooden buildings are the studios of glass blowers, ceramists, weavers, blacksmiths, jewelers and other crafts people, who create the finest examples of modern Norwegian design.

107

Lars Mikael Forselius:
CONSULEN, QUALITY RØROS HOTEL, RØROS

The interior of *Consulen* is reminiscent of the old manors of the mining town. Its name refers to the founder of the hotel, who was Swedish vice-consul at Røros for many years.

Lars Mikael Forselius (b. 1974 in Sweden) trained at *Franska Matsalen* in the world-renowned *Grand Hotel* in Stockholm. He also worked with beer specialist Stefan Thorstensson at *Den Blå Døren* before he came to Røros in 1995. He took over as chef at *Quality Røros Hotel* in 1997, and that also included the well-known gourmet restaurant *Consulen*, the pride of the hotel.

MAIN COURSE
Deer with Chanterelle Sausage, Blueberry Sauce and Root Vegetable Rösti

200 g (8 oz) chanterelles
unsalted butter
salt and black pepper
200 g (8 oz) ground deer meat
1 Tbsp chopped thyme
4 Tbsp (1/4 cup) whipping cream
1 Tbsp cornstarch
1 tsp green pepper berries (canned), crushed
3 Tbsp Cognac
1 tsp juniper berries
30 cm (12") lamb casings

4 dl (1 2/3 cups) concentrated game stock
3 Tbsp Port wine
4 Tbsp (1/4 cup) blueberry purée
1 Tbsp balsamic vinegar
1 Tbsp sugar
2 medium carrots
300 g (10 oz) almond potatoes
1/4 medium celeriac
1/2 medium parsnip
1 parsley root
500 g (1 1/4 lb) strip loin of deer
2 shallots, minced

Sauté 50 g (2 oz) of the chanterelles in 1 1/2 Tbsp butter. Sprinkle with salt. Place in a food processor with ground deer, thyme, cream, cornstarch and pepper berries. Pulse several seconds. Season with 1 Tbsp Cognac, juniper berries and salt. Stuff into lamb casings and tie into four sausages.

Reduce stock with Port and blueberry purée several minutes. Beat in 2 Tbsp butter. Season with vinegar, sugar, the remaining Cognac, salt and pepper.

Slice one carrot. Grate remaining vegetables. Season with salt and pepper. Melt 2 Tbsp butter in a non-stick pan. Pack the grated vegetables in the pan and fry until golden on both sides.

Divide the meat into four pieces of equal size. Grill for 2 minutes per side. Pack in foil and let rest at least 5 minutes before serving. Grill the mushroom sausage.

Sauté sliced carrot with the shallots and the remaining mushrooms. Season with salt and pepper.

Slice the meat on the diagonal and arrange with sausages and carrots on individual plates. Spoon over sauce. Serve with wedges of rösti. 4 servings

APPETIZER

Wild Mushroom Soup with Smoked Bacon, Barley and Mustard Crème Fraîche

2 1/2 Tbsp pearl barley
2 dl (3/4 cup) boiling water

100 g (4 oz) mixed wild mushrooms, sliced
40 g (1 1/2 oz) smoked bacon, diced
2 small shallots, minced
2 Tbsp unsalted butter
6 dl (2 1/2 cups) reindeer, beef or veal stock
2 dl (3/4 cup) whipping cream
2 Tbsp sherry
1 Tbsp fresh lemon juice
1 Tbsp balsamic vinegar
1/2 tsp grated nutmeg
salt and white pepper
2 Tbsp cornstarch stirred into 2 Tbsp cold stock or water

Mustard crème fraîche:
1 dl (scant 1/2 cup) crème fraîche or dairy sour cream
(do not use low-fat soar cream)
1 tsp ground mustard
2 tsp black mustard seeds
1 Tbsp lemon juice
salt and white pepper

Place the barley in a bowl. Pour over the boiling water and soak for 2-4 hours, preferably overnight.

Sauté mushrooms, bacon and shallots in butter in a saucepan. Add stock, cream and barley. Simmer for 10 minutes. Season with sherry, lemon juice, vinegar, nutmeg, salt and pepper. Whisk in the cornstarch mixture and simmer until thickened.

Mustard crème fraîche: Combine crème fraîche and both mustards and whip until stiff. (Sometimes, sour cream first becomes thin and runny, then it forms peaks.) Season with lemon juice, salt and pepper.

To serve, ladle the soup into bowls. Top with a spoonful of mustard crème fraîche. 4 servings

Ptarmigan season is the high point of the year for many Norwegians. About 100,000 hunters take part, but on average, they bag only about five birds each. Here is a cock in its winter feathers, not during hunting season.

MAIN COURSE

Trout-Crayfish Roulade with Whitefish Caviar

800 g (1 3/4 lb) boneless but not skinless trout fillet from the thickest part of the fish
80 g (3 oz) cooked freshwater crayfish meat or crabmeat
3 Tbsp (about 1 1/2) egg white
1 1/2 dl (2/3 cup) whipping cream
1 Tbsp cornstarch
4 Tbsp (1/4 cup) chopped chervil
salt and pepper
1 large shallot, minced
120 g (4 oz) unsalted butter
1 dl (scant 1/2 cup) white wine

4 green asparagus
4 spring onions
100 g (4 oz) snow peas

4 dl (1 2/3 cups) crayfish stock or clam juice
4 Tbsp (1/4 cup) chopped dill
2 Tbsp grated horseradish
2 Tbsp lemon juice
salt and white pepper

80 g (3 oz) whitefish caviar

Trim the fish to make the fillet as rectangular as possible. Purée 200 g (7 oz) of the trout (trimmings plus some cut from the fillet) with the crayfish meat. Add egg whites, half the cream, cornstarch and chervil. Season with salt and pepper.

Skin the fish, leaving it attached at one long end. Spread a thin layer of fish purée where the skin used to be. Roll the fish with the skin to form a roulade.

Sauté the shallot in 1 1/2 Tbsp of the butter in a large frying pan. Add trout roulade, wine, salt and pepper. Cover and simmer slowly for about 8 minutes. Carefully remove from the pan and keep warm.

Blanch the asparagus for 3 minutes in lightly salted water. Add the remaining vegetables and blanch for one minute more. Keep warm.

Combine fish pan juices, crayfish stock and remaining cream. Reduce by half over high heat. Beat in remaining butter and stir in horseradish and dill. Season with salt and pepper. Do not allow the sauce to boil.

Divide the vegetables among four soup bowls. Top with fish. Spoon sauce all around. Garnish with caviar. Serve with almond potatoes. 4 servings

Arne Brimi:
FOSSHEIM TURISTHOTELL:

Fossheim Turisthotell in Lom is known far and wide for its food. The mountain villages in the northern part of the Gudbrandsdal Valley have rich traditions with fish and game. From the days of old to the present, the mountain has provided an important supplement to the local way of life. Ptarmigan and reindeer from nearby areas serve as the basis for great recipes at *Fossheim*.

Since Arne Brimi (b. 1957) became chef at *Fossheim* in 1978, he has had free reign to develop what he calls "Nature's Kitchen." Not only has Brimi given the menus at *Fossheim* a singularly Norwegian touch, he has also become the most Norwegian of all Norwegian chefs, through his books, television appearances, lectures, courses and presentations in Norway and abroad. His broad Lom dialect underlines his local origins and emphasis. Brimi, who is self-taught, is a native of Lom. He believes in using local ingredients in modern dishes. Hunting, fishing and picking edible wild plants give him inspiration and ideas. He always seeks to emphasize the remarkable qualities of the Norwegian kitchen.

DESSERT
Norwegian Kransekake
(Almond Ring Cake)

500 g (1 lb) almonds
500 g (1 lb) confectioner's sugar
3 Tbsp flour
3 egg whites

2 Tbsp melted unsalted butter
semolina (farina or cream-of-wheat)

Frosting:
1 egg white
confectioner's sugar

Scald half the almonds and allow to dry thoroughly. Grind all the nuts together. Combine nuts, sugar and flour. Stir in egg whites to make a stiff dough. Refrigerate overnight.

Preheat the oven to 200C (400F). Brush ring cake pans (can be purchased at specialty stores) with melted butter and sprinkle with semolina. Roll out finger-thick "sausages" and place in the prepared pans. Bake for 10 minutes. Cool in the pans.

Beat the egg white with enough confectioner's sugar to make a stiff frosting. Spoon into a pastry tube with a small opening. Pipe frosting onto on the rings before assembling the cake. Either use frosting to "glue" the rings together, or use sugar syrup (see "spun sugar" in previous recipe).

This almond ring cake is decorated with strawberries and ribbons.

DESSERT
Cone Cookies with Cream
on Marinated Berries

Cookies:
5 dl (2 cups) whipping cream
4 Tbsp (1/4 cup) sugar
4 dl (1 2/3 cups) flour
1 tsp vanilla sugar

Marinated berries:
5 dl (2 cups) water
2 Tbsp honey
6-8 mint leaves
5 dl (2 cups) mixed berries,
  such as lingonberries, black
  currants and raspberries

Spun sugar:
1 1/4 dl (1/2 cup) sugar

Cognac cream:
1 dl (scant 1/2 cup) water
1 1/4 dl (1/2 cup) sugar
1 vanilla bean
4 egg yolks
5 sheets (tsp powdered)
  gelatin
5 dl (2 cups) whipping cream
1 dl (scant 1/2 cup) Cognac

Cookies: Lightly whip the cream and stir in the remaining ingredients. Bake in a *krumkake* or *pizelle* iron and form into cones while still warm.

Marinated berries: Combine water, honey and mint leaves in a saucepan and simmer slowly for 5 minutes to make a syrup. Add lingonberries and black currants while the syrup is still warm. Soft berries, such as raspberries, should be added after the syrup is cold. Marinate overnight.

Spun sugar: Melt the sugar in a low, wide saucepan until light brown. Cool slightly. Do not allow to burn. The pan is still warm, so stir carefully with a wooden spoon. When the sugar begins to form threads, the temperature is just right. Place the cookies on baking parchment and spin sugar threads over the cookies by moving the spoon with the liquid caramel back and forth. If the caramel solidifies, reheat.

Cognac cream: Bring water and sugar to a boil. Split vanilla bean lengthwise and add. Simmer for 10 minutes. Remove from the heat and steep for 1 hour. Remove the vanilla bean and reserve for another use. Reheat the syrup. Whisk the egg yolks, then whisk in the syrup. Place the bowl in a pan of hot water and beat until light and creamy.

Soak the gelatin sheets in cold water (sprinkle powdered gelatin over 2 Tbsp cold water) to soften, about 3 (10) minutes. Squeeze out excess water (disregard for powdered gelatin) and melt. Stir into egg yolk mixture. Whip the cream, fold in the Cognac, then fold into the egg yolk mixture.

Spoon (or pipe) the cream into the pastry cones. Serve on top of the marinated berries. 6 servings

MAIN COURSE
Brimi's Rosy Ptarmigan

breasts of 3 large ptarmigan
bones from ptarmigan or other game birds

Sauce:
1 Tbsp unrefined sugar
2-3 Tbsp red or white wine vinegar
3 dl (1 1/4 cups) ptarmigan or other game stock
3 dl (1 1/4 cups) dairy sour cream

6 almond potatoes
300 g (10 oz) cleaned porcini or button mushrooms
200 g (7 oz) celeriac, cubed
clarified butter
salt and freshly ground white pepper

2 Tbsp unsalted butter
2 tsp cornstarch stirred into 2 tsp cold water (if desired)
fresh herbs

Steam the ptarmigan breasts on a rack over boiling water, covered, for 5-6 minutes. Remove from the heat and allow to rest for 8-10 minutes. Bone the breasts. Make stock from the bones.

Sauce: Melt the sugar in a saucepan. Add the vinegar and boil until almost evaporated. Add stock and sour cream. Reduce until about 4 dl (1 2/3 cups) remain.

Scrub the potatoes and simmer until just tender. Peel and slice.

Slice the mushrooms. Blanch the celeriac cubes in lightly salted water for about 2 minutes. Sauté celeriac and mushrooms in a small amount of clarified butter. Season with salt and pepper. Add the potatoes and heat through, 2-3 minutes.

Just before serving, steam the ptarmigan breasts, covered, for 2-3 minutes. Halve each lengthwise. Reheat the sauce. Whisk in the butter and season with salt. If the sauce is too thin, stir in the cornstarch mixture and cook until thickened. One breast filet, meat from half a bird, is enough for one person as part of a larger menu.

Arrange a bed of vegetables on individual plates. Top with meat and spoon the sauce all around. Garnish with fresh herbs. 6 servings

Berit Kongsvik og Frode Aga:
HALLINGSTUENE, GEILO:

Hallingstuene is right in the middle of Geilo, a popular winter sports resort located at the top of the Hallingdal Valley, 880 meters above sea level. The restaurant is composed of three old-fashioned dining rooms. A roaring fire and rose-painted log walls provide the intimate framework for a meal at *Hallingstuene*. There are both local and national dishes on the menu, with game and kid featured as house specialties.

Berit Kongsvik (b. 1958) and Frode Aga (b. 1955) met when they studied at Åndalsnes. Aga was chef at *Engebret Café* in Oslo, before the couple went to *Sunnfjord Hotell* in Førde. In 1988, they moved to Geilo, and together, they run *Hallingstuene*.

MAIN COURSE
Hallingstuen's Lightly Salted Lamb Shank

6 Tbsp pearl barley

4 lamb shanks (soaked 24 hours in a salt brine)
1 carrot
1/2 kohlrabi or rutabaga
1 small celeriac
butter

Leek sauce:
1 shallot, minced
1 dl (scant 1/2 cup) white wine
5 dl (2 cups) cooking liquid from the lamb shanks
2 dl (3/4 cup) milk
2 dl (3/4 cup) whipping cream
1 large leek, cleaned, rinsed and sliced
salt and pepper

Soak the barley in water overnight.

Place lamb shanks with any vegetable trimmings in a soup pot just big enough to hold all the meat in one layer. Add water to cover. Do not add salt. Bring to a boil. Skim well. Lower heat and simmer slowly until tender, about 2 hours.

Clean the carrot, kohlrabi and celeriac and cut into chunks. Cook in water with a pat of butter until tender. In a separate saucepan, simmer the barley in cooking liquid from the lamb shanks until tender, about 30 minutes.

Leek sauce: Sauté shallot in butter. Add white wine and reduce until almost all the liquid is evaporated. Add stock and reduce by half. Add milk and cream and reduce by half. Sauté the leek in butter. Add to the sauce. Pour sauce into a blender or food processor and purée until smooth. Season with salt and pepper. Just before serving, beat in 2 Tbsp butter.

Serve the lamb shanks in the center of heated plates with the vegetables all around. Spoon the sauce over the meat and vegetables. Top with barley. 4 servings

MAIN COURSE
Traditional Halling Ptarmigan

4 ptarmigan

Ptarmigan sauce:
bones from the ptarmigan
3 dl (1 1/4 cups) water
2 dl (3/4 cup) milk
1 dl (1/2 cup) whipping cream
1 tsp chopped fresh thyme
4 juniper berries
1 1/2 Tbsp butter
3 Tbsp flour
1-2 Tbsp rowanberry or red currant jelly
salt and pepper

Ptarmigan patties:
250 g (9 oz) meat (scraped from the carcass), legs, hearts,
  livers and gizzards
100 g (3 1/2 oz) fresh pork fat
2 Tbsp potato starch
1 egg
2 tsp salt
1 tsp white pepper
1 1/2 dl (2/3 cup) whipping cream
2 Tbsp butter

Vegetables:
100 g (4 oz) celeriac, peeled and sliced
1 Tbsp butter
2 Tbsp whipping cream

100 g (4 oz) Brussels sprouts, cleaned and halved
2 Tbsp chopped onion
2 Tbsp finely chopped bacon
1 Tbsp butter

100 g (4 oz) chanterelles, cleaned and cut into chunks
1 shallot, minced
1 Tbsp butter

1 1/4 dl (1/2 cup) lingonberries
3 1/2 Tbsp sugar

1 tsp chopped fresh thyme
salt and pepper
2 Tbsp butter

Pluck and bone the ptarmigan. Refrigerate the boneless breasts for later use. Remove all meat from the carcass and legs. Set aside for later use.

Ptarmigan stock: Brown the bones in a large pan. Add water, milk, cream, thyme and juniper berries. Simmer for 30 minutes. Strain. Reduce to about 4 dl (1 1/3 cups). If there is less, add water or beef stock up to that amount. Knead butter and flour together and whisk into the stock, stirring constantly. Bring to a boil and simmer for at least 10 minutes. Season with jelly, salt and pepper. Just before serving, beat with an immersion blender until frothy.

Ptarmigan patties: Coarsely grind carcass and leg meat, hearts, livers and gizzards with the pork fat. Add potato starch, egg, salt, pepper and cream. Form into four patties of equal size. Just before serving, sauté in butter on both sides.

Vegetables: Cook celeriac in lightly salted water until tender. Drain, then steam dry. Transfer to a food processor and purée with butter and cream until smooth. Season to taste.

Blanch the Brussels sprouts in lightly salted water for 2 minutes. Drain. Sauté onion and bacon in butter until onion is transparent. Add the sprouts and sauté for 2-3 more minutes. Sauté chanterelles in butter. Season with salt and pepper.

Purée lingonberries and sugar in a food processor for one minute.

Season the reserved ptarmigan breasts with thyme, salt and pepper. Sauté in butter until "medium." Wrap in aluminum foil and allow to rest for 5 minutes before serving.

To serve, arrange one breast and one patty on each plate. Surround with mushrooms, Brussels sprouts and celeriac purée. Spoon sauce around the edge. Serve lingonberry compote and boiled potatoes alongside. 4 servings

Remo Svendsen:
JOTUNSTOGO, BEITOSTØLEN:

Jotunstogo is the name of the restaurant division of *Bitihorn Fjellstue* (Bitihorn Mountain Lodge) at Beitostølen in Valdres. The restaurant itself is really called *Lirypa*. During the last few decades, Beitostølen has become one of the largest resorts in central Norway. During the winter, there are trails for cross-country skiing as well as alpine lifts and runs. During the summer, there are trails for hiking, bicycling and riding, as well as facilities for water sports, hunting and fishing.

Remo Svendsen (b. 1961) is the man in charge at *Jotunstogo*. He rose through the ranks at the *Hotel Continental*, *Holmenkollen Park Hotel* and *Kastanjen* in Oslo before coming to *Jotunstogo* in 1990.

The wood grouse is the largest bird in the Norwegian fauna. Hearing its mating calls in the marshes on a late winter morning at sunrise is an unforgettable experience. But the wood grouse rarely appears on the Norwegian restaurant menu, as few birds are caught.

APPETIZER

Reindeer Mousse with Red Wine Sauce and Sautéed Oyster Mushrooms

250 g (9 oz) reindeer meat, trimmed of all fat and membrane,
* in chunks*
salt and pepper
2 dl (3/4 cup) full-fat milk
2 1/2 dl (1 cup) whipping cream
2 whole eggs + 2 egg yolks

Red wine sauce:
1 1/2 dl (2/3 cup) red wine
2 dl (3/4 cup) game stock
1 tsp rowanberry or red currant jelly
1 tsp cornstarch dissolved in 1 tsp cold stock or water
2 juniper berries
60 g (2 oz) unsalted butter

200 g (8 oz) oyster mushrooms, in bite-size pieces
butter
12 snow peas, topped and tailed
4 Tbsp (1/4 cup) lingonberries
chervil

Place the reindeer in a food processor with 1/2 tsp salt and 2 ice cubes. With the motor running, slowly add milk and purée until smooth. Add cream and eggs and purée 30 seconds. Press through a sieve. Season to taste. Pour into one large or four individual greased baking dishes. Preheat the oven to 110C (230F). Bake in a water bath for about 40 minutes. Let rest for 25 minutes before unmolding. Reheat slightly before serving.

Red wine sauce: Reduce the wine over high heat by three quarters. Add stock and jelly. Reduce by half. Stir in cornstarch mixture and cook until thickened. Season with juniper berries, salt and pepper. Just before serving, beat in the butter. Strain.

Sauté mushrooms in butter. Cook snow peas in lightly salted water with a pat of butter 2-3 minutes.

Serve the warm mousse on individual plates with mushrooms and snow peas. Spoon sauce all around and garnish with lingonberries and chervil. 4 servings

APPETIZER

Warm-Smoked Trout with Cauliflower Cream and Horseradish Dressing

400 g (14 oz) boneless trout fillet
2 1/2 Tbsp sugar
1 Tbsp salt
white pepper
5 Tbsp (1/3 cup) smoking chips

Cauliflower cream:
1 small cauliflower, in florets
1 dl (scant 1/2 cup) milk
salt and white pepper
1 tsp walnut oil
4 Tbsp (1/4 cup) whipping cream
1 Tbsp butter

Horseradish dressing:
2 dl (3/4 cup) dairy sour cream
1 Tbsp sugar
2 Tbsp balsamic vinegar
1 tsp lemon juice
1 Tbsp freshly grated horseradish

lettuce
dill

Rub the fish with sugar, salt and pepper. Place in a plastic bag and refrigerate for at least 3 hours. Rinse with cold water and dry with paper towels. Smoke in a home smoker for 12-15 minutes. If you do not have a smoker, preheat the oven to 180C (350F). Heat a frying pan, then add the chips. When they begin to smoke, place the pan in the oven, with the fish on a rack over the pan. Turn off the oven and smoke the fish for about 15 minutes. After the fish is removed, the odor of the smoke will remain in the oven until it is cleaned.

Cauliflower cream: Cook the cauliflower in milk and lightly salted water until tender. Drain and purée in a food processor until smooth. Season with salt, pepper and walnut oil. Stir in cream and butter.

Horseradish dressing: Combine sour cream, sugar, vinegar and lemon. Season to taste. Just before serving, stir in the horseradish.

Place a mound of cauliflower cream on each plate. Top with fish. Spoon dressing all around. Garnish with lettuce and dill. 4 servings

Øivind Winther Fosvold:
BALAKLAVA, FREDRIKSTAD

Balaklava Gjestgiveri (Balaklava Inn) was once a vicarage in Gamle Fredrikstad (Fredrikstad Oldtown), the best-preserved fortified town in northern Europe. *Balaklava*, which was built in 1801, is an example of a civil servant's residence, furnished with art and antiques of its day. Its name refers to a bloody battle at Balaklava during the Crimean War. When a fight broke out in Fredrikstad one night, it was so violent that a witness called it a "real Balaklava." Even if what happened in Oldtown was mild compared to the real battle, the name stayed. Today, that name refers to food and culture of the highest quality, which has made *Balaklava* known far beyond the county.

Øivind Winther Fosvold (b. 1966) trained at *Hotell Bristol* and at *Østmarkseteren* in Oslo. His cuisine is based on regional traditions, but he also uses many new ingredients. Recently, Fosvold represented Østfold county at a competition in France which focused on European regional kitchens. He placed fourth among the 200 participants.

An aerial view of the old town of Fredrikstad. From inside the best-preserved citadel town in northern Europe, Balaklava *offers excellent food in a cultural setting.*

MAIN COURSE
Sautéed Pike-Perch with Chanterelles and Mussels

700 g (1 1/2 lb) boneless pike-perch fillets, skin on
20 mussels
2 shallots, minced
1 large bunch parsley, chopped
clarified butter
2 dl (3/4 cup) white wine
500 g (1 1/4 lb) almond potatoes
salt and pepper
200 g (8 oz) chanterelles
200 g (8 oz) spinach
2 dl (3/4 cup) whipping cream

Scale the fish, then rinse. Cut into eight pieces of equal size. Scrub the mussels, removing the beards.

Sauté half the shallots and parsley stalks in butter. Add mussels and wine. Steam the shells until they open. Remove the meat, discarding the shells. Strain the cooking liquid.

Preheat the oven to 180C (350F). Scrub the potatoes and cut into 1/2 cm (1/4") slices. Dip in clarified butter and place on an oven tray. Sprinkle with salt and pepper. Bake for about 10 minutes.

Clean the chanterelles and cut into bite-size pieces. Rinse the spinach well and remove any coarse stalks. Sauté mushrooms and remaining shallots in butter. Add cream and reduce until thick. Add mussels. Season with salt and pepper.

Add spinach and parsley to mussel cooking liquid and bring to a boil. Transfer to a food processor and purée until smooth.

Preheat the oven to 200C (400F). Sauté fish, skin side down, in butter over high heat. Sprinkle with salt and pepper. Transfer to a baking dish, skin side up, and bake for about 5 minutes.

Arrange a ring of potato slices on each plate. Place mussels and mushrooms in the center. Top with the fish and spoon spinach sauce all around. 4 servings

MAIN COURSE
Breast of Duck with Zucchini Gratin and Wild Mushroom Sauce

1 zucchini
salt and pepper
2 Tbsp chopped sun-dried tomatoes
2 eggs
2 dl (3/4 cup) crème fraîche or whipping cream
3 Tbsp grated fresh Parmesan cheese
2 Tbsp dried porcini mushrooms
1 shallot, minced
unsalted butter
2 dl (3/4 cup) red wine
1/2 dl (3 1/2 Tbsp) balsamic vinegar
5 dl (2 cups) duck or other poultry stock
1 tsp cornstarch stirred into 1 tsp cold water
3 Tbsp unsalted butter
1 Tbsp honey
1 tsp mustard
1 tsp chopped rosemary
700 g (1 1/2 lb) duck breast, skin on
olive oil

Halve the zucchini lengthwise, then slice. Sprinkle lightly with salt and allow to rest for one hour. Rinse under cold water and dry with paper towels.

Preheat the oven to 160C (325F). Combine zucchini slices with dried tomatoes and divide among four individual baking dishes. Combine eggs, crème fraîche and cheese. Season with salt and pepper. Pour over the vegetables. Bake for about 30 minutes, until set.

Meanwhile, soak the dried mushrooms in hot water to cover for about 10 minutes. Sauté shallots and mushrooms lightly in butter. Add wine and balsamic vinegar and reduce by half. Add duck stock and reduce by half. Season to taste. If the sauce is too thin, stir in the cornstarch mixture and cook until thickened. Beat in the butter.

Combine honey, mustard and rosemary. Brown the duck breast, skin side down, in olive oil. Brush with the honey/mustard mixture. Transfer to a baking dish, skin side up, brush with honey/mustard and bake for 5-8 minutes, depending upon the thickness. Pack in aluminum foil and allow to rest for 10-15 minutes before serving.

Cut the duck breasts into thin slices on the diagonal. Unmold the gratins. Serve with asparagus beans sautéed with garlic and potatoes. 4 servings

DESSERT
Cinnamon Tart with Elderberry Sorbet

Pastry:
1 1/4 dl (1/2 cup) flour
3/4 dl (1/3 cup) sugar
3 1/2 Tbsp unsalted butter
1 egg yolk

Filling:
5 dl (2 cups) whipping cream
2 cinnamon sticks
3 Tbsp sugar

Sorbet:
2 dl (3/4 cup) water
1 1/4 dl (1/2 cup) sugar
1 Tbsp glucose
juice and zest of 1 lemon
2 dl (3/4 cup) concentrated elderberry juice (or other juice)
1 egg white

fresh berries
mint leaves

Pastry: Combine all ingredients in a food processor. Pulse until it just holds together. Form a flat cake and wrap in plastic. Refrigerate for 2 hours. Preheat the oven to 180C (350F). Roll out into a circle on a floured board or press into the bottom of a 22 cm (9") springform pan. Bake for about 30 minutes, until golden-brown.

Filling: Combine cream, cinnamon and sugar in a saucepan and reduce by one-third. The filling will set as it cools. Turn on the oven grill. Strain over the baked pastry and place under the grill for a few minutes to color. Cool.

Sorbet: Combine water, sugar and glucose in a saucepan and bring to a boil. Simmer for 5 minutes. Cool. Add lemon juice and zest and concentrated elderberry juice. Beat the egg white until stiff and fold into the juice mixture. Freeze in an ice cream maker.

Serve wedges of the tart with sorbet. Garnish with berries and mint leaves. 4 servings

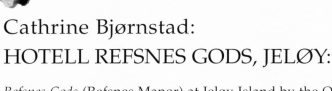

Cathrine Bjørnstad:
HOTELL REFSNES GODS, JELØY:

Refsnes Gods (Refsnes Manor) at Jeløy Island by the Oslo Fjord is built around an old manor house from 1767, and it has been a popular gathering place in the district since that time. A diary entry from the beginning of the 19th century tells of a masquerade ball there with 300 guests. The landscape around Jeløy has attracted many of Norway's great artists. Edvard Munch, Peder Balke and Hans Gude all stayed at *Refsnes*.

Cathrine Bjørnstad (b. 1965) is one of only three female chefs with recipes in this book. At present, they have few colleagues at Norwegian restaurants, but the numbers are expected to rise. Cathrine Bjørnstad trained at *Hotel Continental* in Oslo and took over as chef at *Refsnes Gods* during the summer of 1997.

APPETIZER
Haddock Roulade with Smoked Salmon and Lime Sauce

500 g (1 1/2 lb) boneless and skinless haddock fillet
1 shallot, coarsely chopped
1 Tbsp chopped herbs, such as basil, dill or chives
1 tsp white wine or vermouth
salt and freshly ground white pepper
1/4 tsp anise seed
1/2 dl (3 1/2 Tbsp) whipping cream
1/2 egg white, stiffly beaten
8 small thin slices smoked salmon

Lime sauce:
1 dl (scant 1/2 cup) fish stock
1/2 dl (3 1/2 Tbsp) white wine
shredded zest of 1 lime
juice of 1/2 lime
a few threads saffron
80-100 g (3-4 oz) unsalted
  butter

Potato wafers:
1 medium raw, peeled potato
vegetable oil

Place the fish on a cutting board. You will need a 300 g (10 oz) thin rectangular piece of even thickness for the roulade. Trim the edges and trim horizontally from the thickest part to make 200 g (7 oz) for the filling.

Purée 200 g (7 oz) fish, shallot, herbs, wine, 1 tsp salt and 1/2 tsp pepper in a food processor. With the motor running, add the cream. Fold in the egg white. Place in the refrigerator.

Pound the remaining piece of fish lightly to make it flat and even. Place on greased foil or plastic wrap. Cover with salmon slices. Spread a thin layer of purée over the salmon. Roll up from the long side. Seal the foil well or tie the plastic wrap very well. Simmer in fish stock or water for about 15 minutes.

Lime sauce: Combine stock, wine, lime zest and juice in a saucepan and reduce by half over high heat. Add saffron. Whisk in the butter in pats. Keep warm but do not allow to boil. Season with salt and pepper.

Potato wafers: Coarsely grate the potato and squeeze out the liquid. Sprinkle with salt and pepper. Fry until crisp in a well-oiled *krumkake*, *pizelle* or waffle iron.

Cut the roulade into 12 slices. Arrange three on each plate with sauce all around. Garnish with potato wafers. Serve with carrots and snow peas, if desired. Garnish with fresh basil. 4 servings

MAIN COURSE
Filet of Deer with Chicken Mousse and Chanterelle-Butter Sauce

400 g (14 oz) filet of deer
unsalted butter
salt and pepper

Chicken mousse:
250 g (9 oz) boneless and skinless raw chicken
1 tsp salt
1/2 tsp freshly ground white pepper
3 Tbsp white wine
1 tsp chopped parsley
1 tsp chopped thyme
1 egg
1 1/2 dl (2/3 cup) whipping cream

olive oil

Chanterelle-butter sauce:
80 g (3 oz) chopped chanterelles
2 shallots, minced
1/2 tsp chopped chives
3 dl (1 1/4 cups) rich game stock
100-120 g (3 1/2-4 oz) cold unsalted butter

Brown the meat in butter. Season with salt and pepper. Cool.

Purée chicken, spices, wine and herbs in a food processor. With the motor running, add egg and cream and purée until smooth.

Preheat the oven to 200C (400F). Spread the chicken mixture on a sheet of plastic wrap. Place the deer filet in the center and pack the chicken mixture evenly around it. Remove the plastic. Heat olive oil in a frying pan. Use a narrow spatula to transfer the roulade to the pan. Brown on all sides, then roast in the oven for 10-12 minutes, according to the thickness and desired doneness. Allow the meat to rest for at least 5 minutes before slicing.

Chanterelle-butter sauce: Sauté mushrooms, shallots and chives in 1 Tbsp butter. Add stock and wine. Reduce by half. Whisk in remaining butter in pats. Season with salt and pepper. Do not allow to boil.

To serve, arrange slices of the roulade on individual plates. Spoon sauce all around. Serve with almond potatoes and seasonal vegetables. 4 servings

Picture on following page.

Pål Suarez:
VÆRTSHUSET BÆRUMS VERK:

Since it first opened in 1987, *Værtshuset Bærums Verk* has been considered one of the best restaurants in Norway. The history of the tavern dates all the way back to 1640, when it was opened to maintain some control over the drinking habits of the local laborers. The employees at the nearby ironworks, as well as farmers and traveling peddlers, made it a lively gathering place, while at the same time it played an important social role in the community. Taxes from the sale of spirits went directly to pay relief to the poor and unemployed. The tavern was in operation for 250 years, until around 1890. Later, the building was declared an historic monument and restored with its traditional interior and ambiance very well-preserved.

Pål Suarez (b. 1969) apprenticed at *Park Hotell* in Sandefjord. He has also worked at many of Norway's leading restaurants, including *Holbergs Årstidene*, *Bagatelle* and *D'Artagnan*. He came to *Værtshuset Bærums Verk* in 1996.

MAIN COURSE
Filet of Lamb with Mangold and Olive Purée Served with Natural Juices and Lamb Sweetbreads

600 g (1 1/3 lb) boneless loin of lamb with fat
fresh thyme
salt and pepper
lamb bones (from the boned loin)
olive oil
100 g (4 oz) lamb sweetbreads
4 garlic cloves, peeled
300 g (10 oz) mangold leaves
butter
1 1/4 dl (1/2 cup) black olives, pitted
1 tomato
3 Tbsp unsalted butter

Score the lamb fat. Rub with chopped thyme and sprinkle with salt and pepper. Refrigerate until later.

Chop the lamb bones and brown in olive oil. Add cold water to cover and bring to a boil. Add vegetable parings (if desired), lower heat and simmer for about 4 hours. Strain and reduce over high heat until 3 dl (1 1/4 cups) remain.

Blanch the lamb sweetbreads in boiling water for 20 minutes. Clean, removing all membrane.

Cube the sweetbreads and sauté in oil until golden. Add to the reduced lamb stock.

Blanch garlic in boiling water three times, changing the water each time. Cool, then slice thinly. Make slits in the lamb and insert garlic. Sauté, fat side down, in oil until brown and crispy. Turn and cook until pink. Keep warm.

Cut the mangold into equal lengths and steam in a small amount of lightly salted water with a pat of butter until tender. Keep warm.

Purée the olives in a food processor until smooth.

Scald the tomato in boiling water for about 30 seconds, then peel, seed and chop. Add to the reduced lamb stock. Whisk in the unsalted butter. Do not allow the stock to boil.

Arrange the mangold in the center of heated plates. Slice the lamb and place on the mangold. Top with eggs of olive purée. Spoon a little sauce around the edge of each plate. Serve with boiled potatoes and garnish with fresh thyme. 4 servings

APPETIZER
Sautéed Mackerel with Vegetables and Horseradish Cream

400 g (14 oz) mackerel fillets, skin on
salt and pepper
butter

2 spring onions
4 small carrots
2 small turnips
2 white asparagus stalks
1/2 cucumber
2 dl (1 cup) dry white wine
1 dl (1/2 cup) water
1 1/2 Tbsp unsalted butter

300 g (10 oz) new potatoes
1 dl (1/3 cup) vegetable oil
salt and pepper

1 1/2 dl (2/3 cup) whipping cream
1-2 Tbsp grated horseradish
1 1/2 tsp confectioner's sugar
fresh herbs

Remove any small bones from the fish, but leave the skin on. Cut into four pieces of equal size. Season with salt and pepper.

Cut the vegetables into bite-sized pieces. Combine white wine, water and unsalted butter in a saucepan and bring to a boil. Blanch the vegetables for about 2 minutes. Reheat just before serving.

Scrub the potatoes and cut into wedges. Fry in oil until golden. Sprinkle with salt and pepper.

Whip the cream. Fold in horseradish and confectioner's sugar.

Fry the mackerel on both sides in butter until crispy and cooked through.

Arrange the vegetables on heated plates. Top with fish and place the potato wedges around the edge. Form 8 eggs of horseradish cream with a warm spoon and place on the fish. Garnish with fresh herbs. 4 servings

Trond Moi:
BØLGEN & MOI, HØVIKODDEN:

Bølgen & Moi, in the *Henie-Onstad* Art Center at Høvikodden, near Oslo, enjoys an idyllic setting at the edge of the Oslo Fjord. In just a short time, the restaurant has built up a reputation as one of Oslo's best. Both food and art are on the menu, so that visitors to the museum can combine a cultural experience with a culinary one. *Bølgen & Moi* features informal, modern food with flavors from around the world.

Trond Moi (b. 1969) won the Norwegian championship for chefs in 1995, 1996 and 1997 and he was Fish Chef of the year in 1995. As a member of the Norwegian culinary team, he has won a number of gold and silver medals in international competitions. Moi has worked with Michel Guerard in France, at *Holbergs Årstidene* in Oslo and at the Norwegian Culinary Institute in Stavanger. For Moi, being a chef is a lifestyle in which he rediscovers old traditions, renews them and applies them in the contemporary kitchen.

APPETIZER
Ocean Crayfish Invasion

12 ocean crayfish
salt and freshly ground pepper
2 Tbsp walnut oil
6 ripe tomatoes
1 Tbsp tomato paste
1 Tbsp extra virgin olive oil
1/2 tsp minced fresh ginger
1 tsp red wine vinegar
1 tsp balsamic vinegar
12 green asparagus stalks
1 small lettuce
wine vinegar
oil

Carefully shell and devein the crayfish tails. Sprinkle with salt and pepper. Sauté, red side down, in walnut oil over medium heat for about two minutes.

Scald the tomatoes in boiling water for about 30 seconds, then peel, seed and chop. Combine with tomato paste, oil, ginger and both kinds of vinegar. Season with salt and pepper.

Break off the tough, pale ends of the asparagus stalks. Peel the bottom half. Cook in lightly salted, lightly sugared boiling water for two minutes. Plunge into ice water.

Clean the lettuce in ice water, then spin dry. Arrange the lettuce on a platter. Top with marinated tomatoes, crayfish and asparagus. 4 servings

MAIN COURSE
Bølgen & Moi's Homemade Fish Pudding

500 g (1 1/4 lb) haddock (or other white fish) fillets
1 egg
5 dl (2 cups) whipping cream
1 tsp salt
1 tsp chopped fresh thyme
1 Tbsp chopped fresh lovage
1 Tbsp chopped fresh parsley
1 red bell pepper, chopped
salt and freshly ground pepper
butter
ground sweet paprika
curry powder

Curry sauce:
2 shallots, minced
1 Tbsp butter
1 tsp curry powder
2 dl (3/4 cup) white wine
3 dl (1 1/4 cups) fish stock
3 dl (1 1/4 cups) whipping cream
2 tsp cornstarch dissolved in 2 tsp cold water
salt and freshly ground pepper

Cut the fish into cubes and place in the freezer along with the egg and cream for about 30 minutes. Preheat the oven to 180C (350F). Place fish cubes and salt in a food processor. With the motor running, add the egg and the cream in a thin stream. Add the herbs and the pepper. Process until smooth. Season with salt and pepper. Pour the mixture into a 1 1/2 liter (6 cup) terrine or loaf pan. Brush the top with melted butter. Bake for 20-25 minutes. Cool completely.

Curry sauce: Sauté the shallots in butter with the curry powder. Add the wine and reduce by half. Add cream and stock and reduce by half. If the sauce is too thin, stir in the cornstarch mixture. Bring to a boil, then season with salt and pepper.

Just before serving, cut the pudding into 2 cm (3/4") slices. Season with paprika and curry powder and fry in butter until golden. Serve the pudding with crispy potatoes, buttered vegetables and curry sauce. Layer vertically, so there will be some height to the dish. Garnish with herbs. 6 servings

DESSERT
Lemon-Vanilla Cheesecake

Crust:
15 Kornmo crackers, broken (1 1/3 cups graham cracker crumbs)
3/4 dl (1/3 cup) sugar
120 g (4 oz) unsalted butter

Filling:
1 vanilla bean
1 lemon
700 g (1 1/2 lb) unflavored cream cheese
1 1/2 dl (2/3 cup) sugar
4 eggs

Topping:
1 vanilla bean
5 dl (2 cups) dairy sour cream
1 dl (scant 1/2 cup) sugar

Crust: Preheat the oven to 180C (350F). Pulse all ingredients in a food processor until well blended. Press into the bottom of a 26 cm (10") springform pan. Bake 10 minutes.

Filling: Lower the oven temperature to 140C (280F). Split the vanilla bean lengthwise and scrape out all the seeds with a knife. Reserve the bean itself for another use. Place vanilla, lemon, cream cheese, sugar and eggs in a large mixer bowl. With an electric mixer, beat until well-combined. Pour over the crust. Bake for about 25 minutes.

Topping: Split the vanilla bean lengthwise and scrape out all the seeds. Reserve the bean for another use. Whisk together vanilla seeds, sour cream and sugar. Carefully pour over the cheesecake as soon as it comes out of the oven. Do this slowly, so that the pressure of the topping does not make a crack in the cheesecake. Cool on a rack. The topping is supposed to be runny while warm. It sets as the cake cools. Refrigerate overnight before serving.

Fresh fruit and berry sauces both look and taste good with this cheesecake.

Lucien Mares:
LE CANARD, OSLO:

Le Canard is one of the Frogner-restaurants with a *Michelin* star. It is housed in one of Oslo's most interesting buildings, built more than 100 years ago as the mansion of a wealthy family. It is decorated with sculptures, ornaments and other decorations by turn-of-the-century Norwegian artists. Well-known artists are still part and parcel of *Le Canard*. Danish artist Bjørn Wiinblad designed the cover of the menu, while Hans Normann Dahl did a drawing of the building for it.

Lucien Mares (b. 1955 in Belgium) worked in London before he came to Oslo in 1985 to work at the artists' restaurant, *Blom*. In 1992, he became chef at *Le Canard*.

*Frogner Park, with Gustav Vigeland's many monumental sculptures, is Norway's most popular tourist attraction. But Frogner is also the gastronomic center of Oslo. Three of the four Norwegian restaurants with **Michelin** stars are located in this relatively small area, as well as more than 30 other places to dine. There's something for everyone in every price category in Frogner.*

APPETIZER

Salad with Marinated Duck Breast and Grilled Jerusalem Artichokes

2 duck breasts, about 300 g (10 oz) each, fat removed
olive oil

Marinade:
1 tomato
1/2 green bell pepper
1/2 yellow bell pepper
1 small red onion
1 Tbsp capers
12 black olives
1 garlic clove
2 dl (3/4 cup) extra virgin olive oil
2 Tbsp balsamic vinegar
1/4 tsp cayenne pepper

200 g (8 oz) Jerusalem artichokes
fresh thyme

Preheat the oven to 200C (400F). Season duck breasts with salt and pepper. Brown on both sides in olive oil. Transfer to the oven and roast for around 3 minutes. Cool.

Scald the tomato in boiling water for about 30 seconds, then peel, seed and dice. Clean and julienne the peppers and onion. Combine with remaining ingredients for marinade. Add the duck breasts. Cover with plastic wrap and refrigerate for 24 hours.

Peel the Jerusalem artichokes and cut into thick slices. Blanch for two minutes in lightly salted water. Brush with oil and sauté in a grill pan until tender.

Cut the marinated duck breasts into thin slices. Arrange on individual plates. Top with the marinated vegetables and drizzle over 2 Tbsp of marinade. Serve the grilled artichoke slices alongside. Garnish with thyme.
4 servings

APPETIZER
Sautéed Scallops Le Canard

1 smoked duck breast
12 sea scallops (without roe)
8 chanterelles
salt and pepper
3 Tbsp walnut oil
1 shallot, chopped
3 Tbsp white wine
2 dl (3/4 cup) duck stock
12 walnut halves
chives

Cut the duck breast lengthwise into long thin slices. Wrap two slices around each scallop and thread onto wooden saté sticks or skewers, three scallops alternating with two chanterelles per stick. Season with salt and pepper. Heat 1 Tbsp walnut oil in a frying pan and sauté the scallop sticks on both sides. Remove from the pan and keep warm.

Sauté shallot in the same pan until golden, then add the wine and reduce until 1 Tbsp remains. Add the duck stock and reduce by half. Stir in the remaining walnut oil and season with salt and pepper.

Remove the scallops and mushrooms from the skewers and arrange on individual plates. Strain the sauce over. Garnish with nuts and chives. 4 servings

MAIN COURSE
Sautéed Lobster Flavored with Ginger and Cumin

Court bouillon:
5 liters (quarts) water
1 dl (scant 1/2 cup) sea salt
2 carrots, sliced
1 medium onion, sliced
1 clove
2 branches fresh thyme
2 bay leaves
1 Tbsp white peppercorns
1 garlic clove

4 lobsters, 450 g (1 lb) each

Ginger-cumin oil:
1 dl (1/3 cup) vegetable oil
1/2 tsp ground cumin
1 tsp grated fresh ginger
2 sprigs lemon-thyme
1 bay leaf

Parsley oil:
60 g (2 oz) chopped parsley
1 shallot, chopped
1 garlic clove, chopped
1 1/2 dl (2/3 cup) extra virgin olive oil
salt and freshly ground pepper

100 g (4 oz) snow peas
100 g (4 oz) yellow squash
16 shiitake mushrooms

Court bouillon: Place all ingredients in a large pot and bring to a boil. Simmer for 20 minutes. Add lobsters and simmer for 7 minutes. Remove from the pot and cool quickly. Remove meat from tail and claws. Reserve the head for garnish.

Ginger-cumin oil: Heat all ingredients to 70C (140F) and steep for about 20 minutes. Strain.

Parsley oil: Place parsley, shallot and garlic in a food processor. With the machine running, slowly add the olive oil until emulsified. Season to taste.

Julienne the snow peas and squash. Blanch in lightly salted water for 2 minutes. Sauté in parsley oil with the mushrooms.

Heat the ginger-cumin oil in a frying pan and lightly sauté the lobster meat.

Preheat the oven to 180C (350F). Heat the lobster head until warm, about 10 minutes.

To serve, divide the vegetables among four individual plates. Top with lobster. Drizzle parsley oil all around. Garnish with the lobster heads. 4 servings

Lars Erik Underthun:
RESTAURANT FEINSCHMECKER, OSLO:

Restaurant Feinschmecker also has a star in the *Guide Michelin*. This cozy restaurant in Frogner has a combination of ambiance and exquisite food which makes a dinner a special experience. The dishes which emerge from *Feinschmecker*'s kitchen are a pleasure for both the eye and the palate, perfect meals made with perfect ingredients.

Lars Erik Underthun (b. 1957) can be considered a veteran on the Norwegian restaurant scene. He was Chef of the Year in 1987, while he was at *Holbergs Årstidene*. He trained at *Hotel Continental*, and for eight years after that, he worked with one of the Norwegian kitchen's "grand old men," Hroar Dege, at *Tre Kokker*, now called *Det blå kjøkken* (The Blue Kitchen) in the Industry and Export Complex on Drammensveien in Oslo.

Lars Erik Underthun won the silver at the unofficial world championships for chefs, Bocuse d'Or *in Lyon in 1991.*

MAIN COURSE
Mustard and Herb-Crusted Lamb

Sauce:
2 dl (3/4 cup) dry white wine
5 dl (2 cups) lamb stock
1 Tbsp cornstarch dissolved in 1 Tbsp cold water
2 1/2 Tbsp unsalted butter
salt and pepper

700 g (1 2/3 lb) boneless lamb strip loin, fat and
   membranes removed
butter
vegetable oil
1 Tbsp chopped fresh thyme
2 Tbsp Dijon mustard
1 dl (1/3 cup) chopped parsley
300 g (10 oz) fresh pasta or noodles
1 dl (1/3 cup) whipping cream

Sauce: Reduce the white wine by half. Add stock and reduce by half. Whisk in the cornstarch and cook until thickened. Just before serving, whisk in the butter. Season with salt and pepper. Do not allow to boil.

Preheat the oven to 180C (350F). Brown the lamb on all sides in a mixture of butter and oil. Transfer to an oven pan. Season with salt, pepper and thyme. Brush with mustard and sprinkle with parsley. Roast for 15 minutes. Remove from the oven and allow to rest for 15 minutes. Reduce the oven temperature to 150C (300F) and roast for 5 more minutes. Let rest for several minutes before slicing.

Meanwhile, cook the pasta in lightly salted water. Bring the cream to a boil and fold in the finished pasta. Season to taste.

Slice the lamb on the diagonal and arrange on a bed of pasta. Spoon the sauce all around. Serve with buttered seasonal vegetables. 4 servings

MAIN COURSE
Fillet of Mackerel in Herb Bouillon with Vegetables and Horseradish

4 mackerel, about 400 g (14 oz) each
5 dl (2 cups) fish stock
3 dl (1 1/4 cups) dry white wine
1 bay leaf
2 shallots, sliced
1 carrot, julienned
1/4 celeriac, julienned
1/4 leek, julienned
salt and freshly ground white pepper
1 Tbsp unsalted butter
1 Tbsp extra-virgin olive oil
1 Tbsp chopped parsley
1 Tbsp chopped chives
1 Tbsp freshly grated horseradish
fresh herbs

Fillet the fish, removing all bones. Rinse and dry well. Halve each fillet diagonally. Bring stock and wine to a boil. Add bay leaf, shallots and vegetables. Simmer for 2 minutes, then add the fish and simmer until firm, 5-6 minutes. Transfer fish to deep bowls. Remove the vegetables with a slotted spoon and arrange over the fish. Return the stock to a boil. Skim well. Season with salt and pepper. Beat in butter and olive oil. Add parsley and chives and pour over the fish. Sprinkle with horseradish and garnish with fresh herbs. Serve immediately.
4 servings

DESSERT
Rhubarb with Vanilla Cream and Sauternes Aspic

400 g (14 oz) red rhubarb
2 dl (3/4 cup) water
1 1/4 dl (1/2 cup) sugar
1/4 vanilla bean, split

Vanilla cream:
5 dl (2 cups) milk
1/2 vanilla bean, split
5 egg yolks
1 1/4 dl (1/2 cup) sugar
2 Tbsp cornstarch

1/4 vanilla bean, split
1 dl (scant 1/2 cup) Sauternes wine
2 sheets (tsp powdered) gelatin

1 dl whipping cream
fresh mint leaves

Peel the rhubarb and cut into 3 cm (1 1/4") pieces. Simmer water, sugar, rhubarb peelings and the seeds scraped from the inside of the vanilla bean a few minutes. Strain. Add rhubarb and bring to a boil. Remove from the heat. Allow to cool.

Vanilla cream: Bring milk and vanilla seeds to a boil. Whisk together egg yolks, sugar and cornstarch. Whisk the milk into the egg mixture and return to the saucepan. Bring to a boil and simmer, stirring constantly, for one minute. Pour into a bowl and allow to cool.

Remove the rhubarb from the syrup and set aside. Bring syrup and vanilla seeds to a boil. Reduce by half. Add wine and simmer for several minutes. Strain and allow to cool.

Soak the gelatin sheets in (sprinkle the powdered gelatin over 1 Tbsp) cold water to soften, about 5 minutes. Squeeze excess water from gelatin sheets (disregard for powdered gelatin) and melt over low heat. Stir into the Sauternes syrup. Refrigerate until slightly thickened.

Whip the cream. Whisk the vanilla cream until smooth, then fold in the whipped cream. Divide among four bowls. Arrange the rhubarb over the vanilla cream and refrigerate a few minutes. Carefully pour the gelatin mixture over the rhubarb. Refrigerate for at least 30 minutes before serving. Garnish with mint leaves.
4 servings

Harald Osa:
THEATERCAFÉEN, OSLO:

Hotel Continental has a special place in Norwegian hotel and restaurant life. This family hotel was first opened in 1900, and has been run by the same family for four generations. *Hotel Continental* is right in the center of everything, with the National Theatre across the street, and the Palace, Storting (parliament), City Hall, the Aker Brygge shopping and entertainment complex and Oslo's promenade street, Karl Johan, all within walking distance. The prestigious restaurant *Annen Etage* (Second Floor), which was the hotel's flagship and an institution in Oslo, has been closed for several years, but it is due to reopen in the autumn of 1998. Few doubt that *Annen Etage* will once again become a favorite for Oslo restaurant-goers.

But *Theatercaféen* has never been closed. The cafe is an important cultural institution and Oslo's most popular meeting place, where young and old alike go to see and be seen. Few restaurants can compare with *Theatercaféen*. The *New York Times* included it in its list over the ten most famous cafes in the world, and authors and journalists from abroad have written that *Theatercaféen* alone makes Oslo worth a visit.

Harald Osa (b. 1958) has become a central figure in the Norwegian kitchen. During his seven years as head of the Gastronomic Institute in Stavanger, he shaped it into a leading institution in Norwegian cuisine. In 1998, he succeeded the legendary Willy Wyssenbach as chef de cuisine at *Hotel Continental*, one of the most prestigious positions in the restaurant profession in Norway. Osa has served many stints in France and was chef at *Jans Mat og Vinhus* in Stavanger. He was chef of the year in 1986 and was a member of the Norwegian Culinary Team as well as its leader over many years. He has written several cookbooks and is a popular guest on Norwegian television. Norwegian organizations has through many years made use of his talents to showcase Norwegian cuisine abroad.

APPETIZER
Shrimp Salad with Orange-Basil Dressing

1 red bell pepper
1 bunch chives
350 g (12 oz) cooked shelled tiny shrimp

Dressing:
1 large orange
1 dl (1/3 cup) extra virgin olive oil
20 fresh basil leaves
salt and pepper

mixed lettuce leaves

Clean pepper and cut into small dice. Chop the chives. Combine with the shrimp.

Peel the orange. Do not leave any white membrane. Cut into filets and place in a food processor with oil, basil and salt and pepper. Process until smooth. If the orange is too sweet, add a little lemon juice. If the orange is too sour, add a little sugar.

Combine sauce with the shrimp mixture and serve on lettuce leaves. 4 servings

I don't look forward to traveling any more. I was convinced that there were no new places in the world to discover. But I hadn't counted on Theatercaféen in Oslo, which I had never heard of. Try to imagine a café with an atmosphere that's a mixture of Sardi's, Elaine's and The Russian Tea Room. Imagine further – I know it's not easy – a room which is larger and holds more tables than all three of those places together, and which is more lively and crowded at all times than the other three at their busiest, and which still is a comfortable place to be, intimate and relaxed, and you have Theatercaféen.

Josep Heller in The New York Times Magazine

MAIN COURSE
Lamb Fricassee with Dill

800 g (1 3/4 lb) boneless lamb   *1 small celeriac*
2 Tbsp chopped fresh dill   *2 onions*
salt and pepper   *1 leek*
2 carrots   *1 Tbsp butter*
2 parsley roots   *1 1/2 Tbsp flour*
2 dl (3/4 cup) whipping cream

Cut the lamb into chunks and place in a pot. Add cold water to cover the lamb by 5 cm (2″). Slowly bring to a boil. Skim well. Add 1 Tbsp dill and salt. Simmer one hour, or until meat is tender. Transfer the meat to a bowl. Pour over a small amount of stock and cover with plastic wrap.

Clean and peel the vegetables and cut into chunks. Cook each separately in lamb stock until tender. Dip the leek into the stock for a few seconds.

Knead butter and flour together and whisk into the hot stock. Whisk until thickened. Add remaining dill and cream. Simmer for a few minutes. Season with salt and pepper.

Serve meat and vegetables on individual plates or in a casserole. Ladle over the sauce. Serve with boiled potatoes. 4 servings

DESSERT
Apple Cake

8 large sour apples
4 eggs
3 1/2 dl (1 1/2 cups) sugar
1 1/3 cups flour
1 tsp cinnamon
1 tsp grated lemon zest
3 1/2 Tbsp melted butter

Preheat the oven to 170C (350F). Grease a 24 cm (9″) springform pan. Peel and core the apples. Cut into large wedges. Beat eggs and sugar until light and lemon-colored. Fold in the flour, cinnamon and lemon zest. Carefully fold in the melted butter. Pour into the prepared pan. Press the apple wedges into the batter. Bake for 40-50 minutes. Serve warm with whipped cream or ice cream. 10 servings

Bent Stiansen:
STATHOLDERGAARDEN, OSLO:

Statholdergaarden is the Norwegian restaurant most recently awarded a star in *Guide Michelin*. The beautiful interior is decorated in the style of the 18th century. The restaurant extends over five small rooms with some of northern Europe's finest stucco ceilings. *Statholdergaarden*'s menu is a mirror of the seasons, and although the ingredients are Norwegian, they are spiced with European trends.

Statholdergaarden was built by Peter Grüner in 1640. After it was taken over by Ulrik Fredrik Gyldenløve, King Frederick III illegitimate son, the estate entered Norwegian history and became the center of society in Christiania during Gyldenløve's life, from 1680 to 1699. Naval hero Peter Wessel Tordenskiold visited many times after Gyldenløve's son took over the house during the 1700's. The rooms where he lived are now part of the restaurant.

Bent Stiansen (b. 1963) is Norway's only world champion in cooking. He won that title at the *Bocuse d'Or* competition in Lyon in 1993. Stiansen trained at *Hotel Continental*, where he took over as chef at *Annen Etage* at the age of 23. That set a standard which he has held ever since. He became Norwegian champion in 1990 and was a member of the Norwegian culinary team from 1988 to 1992. Stiansen owns and runs *Statholdergaarden* together with his Danish-born wife Annette.

APPETIZER
Wild Mushroom Soup with Sautéed Ocean Crayfish Tails, Chanterelles and Chervil

8 ocean crayfish tails
20 small chanterelles
unsalted butter

300 g (10 oz) wild mushrooms
2 Tbsp butter
3 Tbsp chopped shallot
2 garlic cloves, minced
1 Tbsp lemon juice
2 dl (3/4 cup) white wine
5 dl (2 cups) fish stock
2 1/2 dl (1 cup) whipping cream
salt and pepper
2 Tbsp chopped chervil

Shell and devein the crayfish tails. Clean the chanterelles. Sauté crayfish and chanterelles lightly in butter.

Clean the wild mushrooms and cut into thin slices. Sauté in butter with shallots and garlic. Add lemon juice, wine and stock. Reduce over high heat until about one third of the original amount remains. Add cream. Bring to a boil and season with salt and
pepper. Transfer to a food processor and purée until light and frothy.

Serve in soup cups. Garnish with crayfish tails, chanterelles and chopped chervil. 4 servings

MAIN COURSE
Mussel Galette with Pumpkin and Curry Sauce

100 g (4 oz) fresh spinach
1 kg (2 1/4 lb) fresh blue mussels
1 Tbsp butter
1 Tbsp minced onion
1 garlic clove, minced
1 dl (1/2 cup) white wine
150 g (5 oz) skinless and boneless trout fillet
1 egg white
1 dl (scant 1/2 cup) whipping cream
salt and pepper

1 sheet filo pastry or 1 spring roll wrapper
2 Tbsp vegetable oil

3 Tbsp breadcrumbs
3 Tbsp sesame seeds
3 Tbsp flour
1 egg white
vegetable oil

Sauce:
1/4 small apple
1/2 Tbsp curry powder
2 Tbsp butter
2 dl (3/4 cup) mussel stock
2 dl (3/4 cup) whipping cream

4 Tbsp (1/4 cup) pickled pumpkin, cubed
fresh chervil

Clean the spinach, removing any large stalks. Blanch for 30 seconds in boiling water. Chop, then set aside.

Scrub the mussels, removing the beards. Melt the butter in a large pot. Add onion, garlic, mussels and white wine. Cover and bring to a boil. Cook until the shells open, about 5 minutes. Remove the meat from the shells and reserve. Strain the stock and reserve.

Cube the trout and place in the food processor. With the motor running, add the egg white and cream. Season with salt and pepper. Combine the fish purée with half the mussels and the chopped spinach.

Cut the filo pastry into 4 circles and place the purée in the center. Form into flat cakes, about 2x4 1/2 cm (1x2"). Press to flatten and sauté in oil over medium heat for about 3 minutes per side.

Combine breadcrumbs and sesame seeds. Dip the remaining mussels in flour and egg white, then into the breadcrumb/sesame seed mixture. Thread onto saté sticks. Heat the oil in a deep-fryer to 170C (350F) and deep-fry until golden. Season with salt.

Sauce: Sauté apple, onion and curry in butter. Whisk in the reserved stock. Reduce by half. Stir in the cream. Using an immersion blender, whisk until frothy.

To serve, divide each mussel packet in two. Stick in a mussel spit. Garnish with pickled pumpkin and chervil. Drizzle curry sauce all around. 4 servings

MAIN COURSE
Medallions of Cod with Spring Onions and Black Salsify in Red Wine Sauce

Red wine sauce:
3 dl (1 1/4 cups) red wine
1/2 onion
1 Tbsp concentrated beef stock
1 Tbsp sugar
salt and pepper
1/4 tsp cornstarch dissolved in
  1/2 tsp water

Chive butter sauce:
2 Tbsp chopped shallots
2 Tbsp butter
1 dl (1/2 cup) white wine
1 dl (1/2 cup) fish stock
150 g (2/3 cup) cold unsalted
  butter
salt and pepper
lemon juice
3 Tbsp chopped chives

300 g (10 oz) black salsify
vegetable oil

4 cod medallions from the
  thickest part of the fish, about
  150 g (5 oz), skin on
salt and pepper
2 Tbsp vegetable oil
2 Tbsp lime juice
2 Tbsp honey
1 tsp crushed black pepper

8 spring onions, chopped
2 Tbsp butter

Red wine sauce: Combine red wine, onion and beef stock in a small saucepan and reduce over high heat until about 3 Tbsp remain. Season with sugar, salt and pepper. If the sauce is too thin, stir in the cornstarch mixture. Cook until thickened. Keep warm. Add a little water if too much evaporates.

Butter sauce: Sauté shallot in butter. Add wine and stock and reduce over high heat by two-thirds. Beat in cold butter in pats. Do not allow sauce to boil. Season with salt, pepper and lemon juice. Keep warm. Just before serving, stir in the chives.

Scrub the salsify. Do not peel. Cut thin strips with a potato peeler. Heat oil to 140C (375F) and fry until crispy. Drain on paper towels.

Dry the fish medallions with paper towels and sprinkle with salt and pepper. Sauté in oil for about 2 minutes per side. Combine lime juice, honey and pepper and brush on the cod skin.

Cook spring onions in a small amount of salted water with a pat of butter. Drain well.

Place the onions in a circle on each plate. Top with fish. Spoon butter sauce around the spring onions and spoon a ring of red wine sauce around the outer edge. Top with salsify and garnish with chives. 4 servings

Eyvind Hellstrøm:
RESTAURANT BAGATELLE, OSLO:

At the beginning of Bygdøy Allé, a promenade street lined with chestnut trees, *Bagatelle* is an oasis in a busy world. It is not by chance that our journey ends here. There is no better climax for this culinary odyssey than *Bagatelle*, for according to many writers and gourmets both at home and abroad, it is not only the finest restaurant in Oslo, but also in all of Scandinavia. In 1986, Bagatelle was the first restaurant in Norway with a Norwegian chef to be awarded a *Michelin* star. The food there has never been better. The special five and seven-course menus change daily and reveal a kitchen in continuous development. Fish and shellfish have always been Bagatelle's specialties, but everything which comes out of the kitchen is top class.

Eyvind Hellstrøm (b. 1949) has accomplished miracles since he took over *Bagatelle* in 1982. After many years in France, he returned home inspired to make the little neighborhood restaurant into one of Scandinavia's best. He has maintained his high standards throughout his 15 years there, and the dishes emerging from his kitchen taste every bit as good as they look.

APPETIZER

Small Pollack with Caviar and Scallops in Pepper Sauce

100 g (4 oz) celeriac, cleaned and julienned
unsalted butter
20 snow peas, topped and tailed
20 asparagus tips
1 Tbsp minced shallots
2 dl (3/4 cup) white wine
4 dl (1 2/3 cups) fish stock
1 dl (scant 1/2 cup) whipping cream
salt and freshly ground white pepper

400 g (14 oz) boneless and skinless small pollack fillets
4 Tbsp Russian (or other) caviar
4 sea scallops, in thin slices

Cook the celeriac in a small amount of lightly salted water with a pat of butter for one minute. Add the snow peas and cook for one minute more. Blanch the asparagus for about 3 minutes in lightly salted water. Just before serving, reheat in a small amount of butter.

Sauté the shallots in a small amount of butter until transparent. Add wine and reduce over high heat until about one-fourth of the original amount remains. Add fish stock and reduce by half. Add cream and reduce until sauce thickens. Strain and return to the saucepan. Whisk in 3 1/2 Tbsp unsalted butter in pats. Season with salt and pepper. Do not allow the sauce to boil.

Preheat the oven grill. Steam the fish, covered, on a rack over boiling water for about 3 minutes. Transfer to a baking sheet. Top with caviar and scallop slices. Place under the grill for about 2 minutes.

Place celeriac, snow peas and asparagus in the center of four plates. Top with the fish. Spoon the sauce all around. Garnish with dill. 4 servings

DESSERT

Strawberry Cappuccino

1 liter (4 cups) strawberries
2 dl (3/4 cup) water
3/4 dl (1/3 cup) sugar
1 vanilla bean, split lengthwise
1 tsp minced fresh ginger
1/2 cinnamon stick

1 star anise
1 tsp coriander seeds
2 tsp dried orange peel
3/4 dl (1/3 cup) dry fine breadcrumbs
1 1/2 Tbsp brown sugar

2 dl (3/4 cup) whipping cream

Preheat the oven to 70C (160F). Line a cookie sheet with baking parchment. Hull and slice the berries. Spread one-fourth of the berries over the lined cookie sheet and dry in the oven for 2 hours. Check after 1 1/2 hours. They should not change color.

Bring water, sugar, vanilla bean, ginger and cinnamon to a boil. Strain, discarding spices. Add remaining berries and simmer for 10 minutes. Strain. Mix berries with 1 dl (scant 1/2 cup) of the syrup (reserve the rest for sauce) and press through a sieve. Freeze in an ice cream machine or pour into a mold and freeze (then whirl in a food processor just before serving).

Crush anise and coriander in a mortar. Add the orange peel. "Toast" in a dry skillet with breadcrumbs and sugar until golden and aromatic.

Whip the cream.

Spoon berry syrup into the bottom of deep bowls. Place a scoop of sorbet in each. Top with whipped cream. Press dried strawberries into the cream. Sprinkle with spiced breadcrumbs. 4 servings

MAIN COURSE

Chicken with Crayfish Tails and Mushroom Fricassee

1 kg (2 1/4 lb) freshwater crayfish
olive oil
2 dl (3/4 cup) whipping cream
3 1/2 Tbsp cold, unsalted butter
salt and pepper

600 g (1 1/2 lb) chicken breasts, about 4 medium, boneless but skin-on
1 Tbsp fresh tarragon leaves

300 g (10 oz) potatoes
3 dl (1 1/4 cups) clarified butter

150 g (5 oz) fresh spinach
unsalted butter
1 tsp sugar
4 garlic cloves
150 g (5 oz) mixed fresh mushrooms
1 1/2 Tbsp minced shallots

Sauté the whole crayfish in oil, covered, for about 10 minutes. Shell the tails and refrigerate. Chop the shells and the rest of the crayfish in the food processor. Sauté the chopped shells in oil, stirring often, until they are a rich dark color. Do not allow to burn. Add the cream and bring to a boil. Skim well. Simmer for 10 minutes. Strain and keep warm. Just before serving, beat in cold butter in pats. Season with salt and pepper.

Season the chicken with salt and pepper. Cover with tarragon leaves. Pack in plastic wrap. Seal, if possible. Simmer slowly in water for 15 minutes. Remove and set aside.

Preheat the oven to 200C (400F). Peel and thinly slice the potatoes. Heat in clarified butter, then place on a baking sheet. Bake until golden, about 2 minutes. Transfer to paper towels. Sprinkle with salt.

Rinse the spinach well and remove any coarse stalks. Blanch in lightly salted water for about 30 seconds. Heat in a saucepan with butter, sugar, salt and pepper. Stir with a garlic clove speared with a fork. Clean and quarter the mushrooms. Sauté with minced shallots and 1 minced garlic clove. Season with salt and pepper. Sprinkle with chives.

Just before serving, reheat the potatoes in the oven and sauté the chicken and crayfish tails in butter with two whole garlic cloves.

Divide the spinach among four plates. Top with mushrooms. Halve the chicken breasts lengthwise and place on the mushrooms. Top with crayfish tails and spoon sauce all around. Garnish with potato slices.
4 servings

Basic recipes

Rösti Potatoes

600 g (1 1/3 lb) potatoes
salt and pepper
1/2 dl (3 1/2 Tbsp) olive oil

Peel and grate the potatoes. Toss with salt and pepper. Heat the oil in a non-stick pan. Add the potatoes and press them into an even layer. Fry over medium heat until brown on both sides. Make sure that the potatoes are cooked through. Serve in wedges. 8 servings

Tomato Concassé

6 small tomatoes
1/2 garlic clove, minced
1 Tbsp chopped fresh basil
1 Tbsp chopped chives
1 Tbsp tomato paste
1/2 dl (3 1/2 Tbsp) olive oil
salt and pepper

Scald the tomatoes in boiling water for about 30 seconds, then peel and halve. Remove seeds with a spoon. Cut into cubes and combine with remaining ingredients. Season with salt and pepper.

Creamy Mushroom Sauce

3 shallots, sliced
250 g (8 oz) mixed wild or domestic mushrooms
3 Tbsp butter
3 dl (1 1/4 cups) beef or chicken stock
2 dl (3/4 cup) whipping cream
2 Tbsp soy sauce
2 Tbsp chopped parsley
salt and pepper

Sauté shallots and mushrooms in butter until soft and shiny. Add stock and cream and reduce by half. Add soy sauce and parsley. Season with salt and pepper.

Fish Forcemeat

500 g (1 1/4 lb) boneless fillets of lean white fish
1 tsp salt
1/2 tsp white pepper
2 eggs
3 1/2 Tbsp whipping cream

This mixture can be used for quenelles, patés and stuffings. It is important that all the ingredients are well/chilled, as the mixture can separate if it becomes overheated or overprocessed.

Cut the fish into cubes and freeze for 20 minutes. They should not be frozen, just ice cold. Purée in a food processor with salt and pepper for about 1 minute. With the motor running, add the eggs, then add the cream in a thin stream, processing until combined.

Sweet and Sour Mushroom and Onion Compote

1 garlic clove, minced
2 shallots, minced
1 small red onion, in wedges
4 1/2 Tbsp butter
100 g (4 oz) mushrooms, sliced
1 dl (1/3 cup) balsamic vinegar
2 Tbsp sugar
1 Tbsp chopped chives
salt and pepper

Sauté garlic, shallots and onions in 1 1/2 Tbsp of the butter. Add the mushrooms and brown lightly. Add vinegar and sugar and reduce until about 1/4 of the original amount of liquid remains. Just before serving, stir in the remaining butter in pats. Add chives and season with salt and pepper. This compote is good with hearty fish and meat dishes. If desired, add stock and use as a sauce.

Fish Stock

1 kg (2 1/4 lb) fish bones and trimmings
water
1 tsp salt
1 bay leaf
1/2 tsp white peppercorns
1/4 medium onion, sliced
1/4 medium leek, sliced
1/8 small celeriac, sliced

Rinse the fish bones and trimmings. Soak 1/2 hour in cold water. Place the bones and trimmings in a pot with cold water to cover, about 1 1/2 - 2 liters (quarts). Bring to a boil and skim well. Add remaining ingredients, lower heat and simmer about 30 minutes. Strain. Reduce to desired concentration. Cool quickly. If using bones from salmon, mackerel or trout, they must be extremely fresh. 1 liter/quart

Light Stock

3 kg (6 1/2 lb) veal or chicken bones
5 liters (quarts) water
2 Tbsp salt
2 onions, sliced
1 carrot, sliced
1/4 celeriac, sliced
10 cm (4") medium leek, sliced
1 bay leaf
1 Tbsp black peppercorns
1 tsp dried thyme

Place the bones in a pot and add the water. Bring to a boil and skim well. Add remaining ingredients and simmer 4-6 hours. Strain and allow to cool. The stock can be stored refrigerated for 4-5 days or it can be frozen for approximately one year. 3 liters/quarts

White Wine Sauce

3 shallots, minced
1 Tbsp butter
2 dl (3/4 cup) white wine
5 dl (2 cups) fish stock
3 dl (1 1/4 cups) whipping cream
salt and white pepper

Sauté shallots in butter until transparent. Add wine and reduce until syrupy. Add stock and reduce until about 1 dl (1/2 cup) remains. Add cream and reduce to desired consistency. Season with salt and pepper. This sauce can be thickened with cornstarch, if necessary. 4 servings

Ice Cream Parfait

200 g (1 cup) sugar
2 dl (3/4 cup) water
12 egg yolks
1 liter (quart) whipping cream
1 tsp sugar

Combine sugar and water in a saucepan and bring to a boil. Lower heat and simmer 5 minutes. Beat egg yolks until light and lemon colored, about 5 minutes. Slowly add the boiling sugar syrup. Beat until the mixture is light and fluffy and has cooled to room temperature. Whip the cream with the sugar and fold into the egg mixture.

For flavored parfait, spices such as vanilla, cinnamon and ginger should be added while the syrup is simmering. Chocolate, honey and liqueurs should be added to the egg cream, just before the whipped cream is folded into the mixture.

Line a 1 1/2 liter (6 cup) mold with plastic wrap. Pour in the parfait mixture and freeze at least 4 hours. Just before serving, dip the form quickly in warm water, then unmold. Wait a minute or two before removing the plastic wrap, to give it time to defrost slightly. Frozen plastic wrap is brittle and can fall apart on the parfait.

Appetizers and Soups

Main Courses

FISH

Photographs
All dishes have been prepared and photographed in Bengt Wilson's studio.

The chefs represented in this book have not prepared their dishes for photography. They have been prepared and styled by Morten Schakenda of the Gastronomic Institute.

Translation and English recipe adaptation by Melody Favish.

Published by
Index Publishing A/S ©
N-0243 Oslo
Telephone: 47 22 92 63 00
Telefax   47 22 92 63 33
E-mail: index@index.no

Project leader: Gunnar Jerman
Graphic total production: PDC Tangen
Cover and grapshic design: Sean Brewer
Paper: 150 g GalerieArt Silk

ISBN 82-7217-092-2